Simon Says PAY ATTENTION!

Help for children with ADHD

3rd Edition

Daniel Yeager, LCSW, RPT-S

Marcie Yeager, LCSW, RPT-S

The authors thank children's book illustrator **Diane Kidd** for bringing Simon and his Coach to life through her delightful drawings. Ms Kidd also drew the cats for the *Cool Down Rating Scale*.

golden path games™

playtherapy@att.net

Simon Says PAY ATTENTION!
Help for children with ADHD

3rd edition

ISBN: 978-0692793718

golden path games™

www.goldenpathgames.com

CONTENTS

Introduction
What Is Executive Function? 1
How Are Executive Function and ADHD Related? 2
Implications for Treatment 3
Jon's Story: Integrating the Concept of Executive Function into ADHD Treatment 4
The Simon Says Program: Integrating EF into an ADHD Treatment Plan 8
The P.L.A.Y. Formula: How It Works..10
For the Coach: How the Simon Says Program Can Help Your Child 12
For Children: Hi! My Name Is Simon and I Have ADHD 14

That's My Cue! (Working Memory)
Rationale and Overview...18
   Play: Introduction and Skills Checklist 20
      Game: ***Simon Says Pay Attention*** 21
   Link: Story: ***The Morning D.J.*** 27
      When Do People Use These Skills in Real Life? 30
      Coach's Report 33
   Assign: Overview...35
     Don't Forget! Cue Cards 37
     Secret-Signal Cues 41
     Wrist Lists 43
     Ready, Set, *GO for It!* 51
   Yahoo! 53

Summary 57

Don't Do It! (Response Inhibition)
Rationale and Overview...60
   Play: Introduction and Skills Checklist 62
      Game: ***Simon Says Don't Do It!*** 63
   Link: Story: ***The Distraction Zapper*** 67
      When Do People Use These Skills in Real Life? 70
      Coach's Report 73
   Assign: Overview 75
     The ON-OFF Switch 77
     Red Light/Green Light 79
     Don't Do It! Cards 81
     The Stay-on-Track Map 85
   Yahoo! 89

Summary 93

Stop, Relax, Think (Cognitive and Behavioral Flexibility)

Rationale and Overview...96

Play: Introduction and Skills Checklist 98

  Game: *STOP, Relax, Focus, GO!* 99

Link: Story: *The Team Player*..103

  When Do People Use These Skills in Real Life? 106

  Coach's Report 108

Assign: Overview...111

  Attention Please! 113

  The Cool Down 117

  Stop and THINK Poster 121

  STOP and "B" Cool Cue Card 125

Yahoo!: 129

Summary 133

I've Got a Plan! (Goal Orientation)

Rationale and Overview 136

Play: Introduction and Skills Checklist 138

  Game: **The *I've Got a Plan!* Game Show** 139

Link: Story: *Have Fun, Get the Job Done* 143

  When Do People Use These Skills in Real Life? 146

  Coach's Report 149

Assign: Overview 151

  Make-Your-Own Game Plan 153

  Encouraging-Words Cue Cards..157

  Beat the Clock! 163

Yahoo! Encouraging Words..165

Summary 169

References

References 170

A Letter from the Authors

A Letter from the Authors 171

What Is Executive Function?

Executive Function (EF) is a term used to describe a unique set of mental abilities. In general, executive functions are a collection of related, yet distinct, abilities that allow the individual to direct and regulate his or her own behavior. Studies have demonstrated that these functions are performed by the pre-frontal lobes of the cerebral cortex.

Some commonly cited executive functions are:

Working Memory: holding information in mind for the purpose of completing a task or activity

Initiating: beginning a task or activity

Behavioral Inhibition: not acting on impulse; appropriately stopping one's activity at a given time

Internalized Speech: using "self-talk" to guide one's behavior and solve problems

Switching Focus: cognitive flexibility, shifting from agenda A to agenda B

Emotional Control: modulating one's emotional response appropriately to the situation or stressor

Self-Monitoring: checking on one's actions during an activity to assure attainment of a goal

Planning: anticipating the future, setting goals, developing steps ahead of time

Organizing: establishing order in an activity or space, carrying out a task in a systematic manner

Sense of Time: keeping track of the passage of time and altering one's behavior in relation to time

Foresight: ability to predict and plan for the future

Goal Orientation: establishing an image of a goal in one's mind and using that internal image to direct one's behavior

These executive functions begin to develop during infancy and continue through adolescence.

With the gradual maturation of executive functions, children become more able to direct and manage their own thoughts, emotions and behavior. As with all aspects of development, there is great variation in maturation of EF, with some children developing more quickly than others.

SUPPORTING THE DEVELOPMENT OF EXECUTIVE FUNCTION

"Executive Functions exist first … in shared and external forms of interaction and gradually become converted to private and internal mental tools."

- *Executive Function and Child Development* (2013)

"Adults play a critical role in supporting, or "scaffolding," the development of these skills, first by helping children complete challenging tasks, and then by gradually stepping back to let children manage the process independently and learn from their mistakes—as they are ready and able to do so."

- *Enhancing and Practicing Executive Function Skills with Children from Infancy to Adolescence* (2014)

How Are Executive Function and ADHD Related?
A New Understanding of ADHD

Researchers in the field of ADHD have advanced varied ideas and models for how executive functions are related to ADHD. We will briefly discuss two of these models, Russell Barkley's and Thomas Brown's.

Types of ADHD:
- Predominantly Inattentive Presentation
- Predominantly Hyperactive-Impulsive Presentation
- Combined Presentation

Russell Barkley Model*
- Barkley limits his model to ADHD, Combined Type.
- Barkley gives primacy to **behavioral inhibition** as the primordial executive function upon which the development of all other executive functions depend.

Barkley identifies the primary executive function as **behavioral inhibition** which includes: inhibiting responses before actually acting them out, interrupting on-going responses, and resisting distractions. Behavioral inhibition lays the foundation for the development of the other executive functions, which he identifies as:
1. **Working Memory:** holding events in one's mind (sense of time, forethought, hindsight, self-awareness)
2. **Internalized Speech:** speech directed toward self (self-questioning, self-directing, generation of rules)
3. **Self Regulation of Affect, Motivation and Arousal** (Arousal refers here to a state in which one is optimally alert, awake, and attentive.
4. **Reconstitution**: creativity and problem-solving ("playing with" ideas and behaviors by taking them apart and re-assembling them to form novel solutions)

Working together, these functions allow for **Behavioral Control**: execution of goal-directed responses, goal-directed persistence, task re-engagement following disruption, sensitivity to response feedback and behavioral flexibility.

ADHD and the Nature of Self-Control (1997)

Thomas Brown Model*
- Brown applies his model to all types of ADHD
- Brown views behavioral inhibition as just one of multiple executive functions.

Brown identifies six different sets of executive functions that are affected in ADHD:
1. **Activation:** organizing, prioritizing, and activating
2. **Focus:** focusing, sustaining, and shifting attention to tasks
3. **Effort:** regulating alertness and processing speed, sustaining effort
4. **Emotion:** managing frustration and modulating emotions
5. **Memory:** utilizing working memory and accessing recall
6. **Action:** monitoring and self-regulating actions

Attention Deficit Disorder: The Unfocused Mind in Children and Adults (2005)

In both models, it is stressed that:

- As the executive functions develop, children become less controlled by external sources and more capable of regulating and directing their own behavior.

- ADHD represents a **delay in the development** of this shift from outer to inner control.

Implications for Treatment:
Provide External Support at the Point of Performance

ADHD as a Disorder of Performance
Barkley states that ADHD should be considered a disorder of **performance** rather than of **knowledge** or **skill** (Barkley, 1997).

- People with ADHD are just as "smart" as anyone else, but due to deficits in the internally represented information and sense of time, they have difficulty applying their knowledge and skills throughout the course of their day-to-day performance.

- Consequently, no matter how smart or talented the child with ADHD may be, he or she is not performing on an even playing field with their peers.

- However, parents and caregivers can help the child compensate for these differences by providing a longer period of *externalized support* (scaffolding) for the development of executive functions.

External Support Provides a More Even "Playing Field"

With external support in place, the child with ADHD is able to **perform** beyond what their actual development would allow. That is, they are able to use their knowledge, skills and abilities on par with their peers, without being as handicapped by slower development of the executive functions. A simple example of externalizing an executive function is one that many of us use on a daily basis: a "to-do" list.

> *When I set out in my car to run errands, rather than relying on my **working memory** (an executive function), I write down a list of things I need to do and use that list to prompt me to initiate the required actions. The list provides an external structure that supports my working memory.*

Provide External Support at the "Point of Performance"
Barkley also emphasizes that, to be most effective, the externalized support should be available at the **point of performance** (Barkley, 1997). The point of performance is the place and time where a particular action needs to take place.

> *Making a list can be helpful in and of itself, as a way of organizing my thoughts about what I need to do. But it will be far more helpful to me if I don't leave it at home. If I have it with me, on my person, or at least in my car, as I navigate the errands to be done that day, it will always be available at the point of Performance–the natural setting in which I need to recall just what it is I need to do next.*

Simon Says Pay Attention: Help for Children with ADHD

The **Simon Says** program presented in this book is based on this understanding of ADHD as a disorder of performance. Because of the importance of using interventions at the **point of performance**, parent and/or teacher participation is an integral part of the *Simon Says* program. The therapist's role is to use his/her clinical skills to help educate and motivate the child, suggest strategies, and provide tools. The coach's role is to provide scaffolding and encouragement as the child uses those strategies and tools **when** and **where** they are needed.

The following article, *Jon's Story*, presents a clinical example of incorporating the concept of executive function into an ADHD treatment plan.

Jon's Story:
Integrating the Concept of Executive Function into ADHD Treatment

On the first weekend of every month, Mia and her ten- year-old son, Jon, visit her parents two hours away. On this Saturday morning, after breakfast, Mia tells John to feed the dog, get dressed, and bring his suitcase (which they packed last night) downstairs. John nods and smiles. He's looking forward to the trip. Fifteen minutes later, Mia is ready to go. As she passes by Jon's room, she sees that his suitcase is still on his bed. She finds Jon in the yard – in his pajamas, playing with the dog.

Mia is exasperated. What is his problem? Yes, he has ADHD, but how hard is it to do three simple things? He loves to go to his grandparents' house. Why is it such a struggle to get him to listen?

As Mia hurries Jon along, she knows how her sister Lynn would answer that question. *Jon is just spoiled. He pays attention when he's playing a video game. You need to be stricter!* Lynn thinks that Jon's failure to comply is due to a lack of motivation – if he wanted to do it, he could. But Mia isn't so sure. She's been consistent with discipline. Mia also knows that Jon feels bad about himself when he doesn't succeed at school or when she constantly fusses at him at home. She knows that he has begun to compare himself to his peers. He seems frustrated with his inability to accomplish simple things that seem effortless for his friends. She has heard him refer to himself as "dumb." She can't understand why Jon doesn't comply with the instructions he receives from adults, but she doesn't think it's a lack of motivation. She knows in her heart that he would comply if he could.

Jon's school counselor has invited Mia to a seminar. The seminar is for parents of children with ADHD and will focus on something called " executive function." Mia has no idea what executive function is, but decides that she will attend the seminar. She is determined to understand her son's difficulty and help him find a way to overcome it.

****

Executive functions are mental processes that give organization and order to our behavior, allowing us to direct our actions through time toward a goal. Executive functions involve mental processes such as:

- Planning for the future, strategic thinking
- Working memory
- Regulating one's level or arousal and motivation'
- Accurately sensing the passage of time
- Internalized language
- Inhibiting actions that interfere with goal completion (interference control)
- Initiating actions to achieve a goal
- Self-monitoring
- Shifting between tasks as needed

As an example of executive functioning in everyday life, let's look back to the previous evening as Mia returns home from work. She picks up the mail and sorts through it. Her favorite magazine is in the stack, and she would love to sink into her recliner and read it. She recalls (working memory) that she needs to make a cake for her mother's birthday. She wants to get the cake baked before she picks up Jon from his friend's house (strategic thinking). She reminds herself (internalized language) how pleased her mother will be with the cake–an old family recipe. She recalls that she was eight years old when she first, with her mother's help, baked the cake. She begins to feel more energized (regulating motivation). As she gets out the recipe, (initiating action) her phone rings. She checks the display and decides not to answer (interference control). She'll return her friend's call after the cake is in the oven (strategic thinking).

While working, Mia recalls a TV show she had planned to watch; she checks the clock and sees that it is time for the show to start. She makes a decision not to watch it (interference control); if she ends up with free time, she would rather use it talking with her friend (sense of time). She slips the cake in the oven, sets the timer, glances at the clock (self-monitoring) and notes that when the cake is ready it will be time to leave to pick up Jon. She decides to clean the kitchen (shifting between tasks) so she can relax and enjoy the rest of the evening (strategic thinking). When the last dish is put away, she returns her friend's call (shifting between tasks). The two friends talk until the timer rings. Then Mia takes out the cake, remembers to turn off the oven (working memory), grabs her purse and goes to pick up Jon.

Mia's executive functions work smoothly and efficiently. Because this functioning occurs without her conscious awareness, she takes it for granted. But the development of these functions took place over time. If we imagine Mia as an eight-year-old using the family cake recipe for the first time, much of her behavior was probably externally directed by her mother. It was a gradual process for her actions and sense of time become internally directed.

Researchers believe that this capacity for self-direction is neurologically based and concentrated in the pre-frontal region of the brain. While relatively little is known about how specific developmental changes in the frontal cortex are related to specific changes in children's executive functions, an increasing number of studies are addressing this topic (Zelazo, 2005).

The following week at the seminar, Mia learns that current research regarding ADHD is moving away from an emphasis on impulsivity and inattentiveness and toward an emphasis on executive functions. The speaker explains that children with ADHD can successfully compete with peers when playing a video game because that activity provides immediate external cues and feedback that help to direct their behavior. But in situations where children must rely on internally represented information and sense of time, the child with ADHD is not competing on an even playing field with his or her peers. Often the child senses this and – no matter how intelligent or talented the child may be – the child feels different, inadequate, or "dumb."

Executive functions involve mental processes such as:
- Planning, strategic thinking
- Working memory
- Regulating one's level of arousal and motivation
- Accurately sensing the passage of time
- Internalized language
- Inhibiting actions that interfere with goal completion (interference control)
- Initiating actions to achieve the goal
- Self-monitoring
- Shifting between tasks as needed

To provide a more even playing field, many experts in the field recommend that individuals with ADHD compensate by using tools that "externalize" the executive functions (Barkley, 1997). The speaker gives a simple example of a way to externalize an executive function. " When I set out in my car to run errands, I write down a list of things I need to do. I could just rely on my working memory, and hope that I remember everything I need to do. But the list is a helpful tool; it gives external support to my working memory."

The speaker also points out that, to be most effective, this external support should be available at the point of performance (Barkley,1997). "Making a list can be helpful in and of itself, as a way of organizing my thoughts about what I need to do," the speaker says. "But it will be a far more helpful tool if I don't leave it at home. If I have it with me in my pocket, it will always be available at the point of performance – when and where I need to remember what to do next."

The speaker ends by quoting ADHD expert Russell Barkley. Barkley believes that the person with ADHD usually has adequate knowledge and skills; the problem is in executing the skills at the time and place where they are required. Barkley suggests that ADHD should be viewed as a disorder of performance and that treatment for ADHD should focus not on teaching new skills but on helping people perform what they already know (Barkley, 1997).

After attending the seminar, Mia decides to take Jon to a therapist. She hopes that the therapist will be able to explain to Jon why he is having difficulty. She also hopes that the therapist will give them some strategies and tools that they can use to help Jon compensate for his difficulties and perform better in his daily activities.

They next talk about why Jon and Mia are there. Mia relates the history of Jon's diagnosis and treatment over the past three years: the trials of medication, the problems with side effects of the medication, the accommodations that the school has provided, and her own attempts to firm up discipline and provide extra structure and support in Jon's day to day life. Both Mia and Jon are tearful as they describe the tension that has seeped into their relationship. As they talk, it is apparent to the therapist that both of them are frustrated with the continued problems related to Jon's ADHD and that both of them feel guilty. Mia wonders what she has done wrong. Jon states that other kids sometimes say he is " dumb" and that he thinks of himself as " bad" when his mother fusses at him.

Barkley believes that the person with ADHD usually has adequate knowledge and skills; the problem is in executing the skills at the time and place where they are required. Barkley suggests that ADHD should be viewed as a disorder of performance and that treatment for ADHD should focus not on teaching new skills but on helping people perform what they already know (Barkley, 1997).

When they arrive at the therapist's office for the first visit, Mia is a bit taken aback when the therapist introduces herself as a play therapist. If there is one thing Jon loves to do, it is play–what Mia wants the therapist to do is to help him get serious and be more responsible.

The therapist explains that play is a natural and developmentally appropriate way that children practice regulating their behavior. In many children's games – Red Light Green Light, Mother May I, Statues, Simon Says, Freeze Tag – the primary objective of the game is for the players to exercise behavioral inhibition. In other childhood games, the child must rely on working memory. Traditional childhood games, while fun, also provide an engaging external framework for children to practice behaviors that are central to executive functioning.

The therapist comments that they have been doing lots of good things. The treatment that they have already set up–medication, school accommodations, and behavior management–are exactly the kind of things that research has shown to be effective in helping individuals with ADHD. One thing that they might want to add to their treatment plan, the therapist says, is for Jon to become a working member of the " treatment team." Up until now, his treatment has been managed by his physician, his teachers and his mother. The therapist explains that she helps children to become partners in finding solutions to their ADHD-related difficulties. She assures Jon that he is neither dumb nor bad. In fact, he already has lots of knowledge, talent, and skills that he can use to help solve the problems that he is having.

To demonstrate, the therapist gets both Jon and Mia on their feet, playing a variation of the traditional childhood game of Simon Says. In the course of playing the game, Jon and Mia compete with one another, laugh and joke, and smile and relax. The therapist notices that Jon is able to hold information in working memory and, in response to certain cues, initiate required behaviors while inhibiting other behaviors. Jon wants to play the game again and this time the therapist adds more cues, representing different required behaviors, making the game more challenging.

Several rounds and much laughter later, the therapist explains the concept of working memory to Jon. She points out that everyone is different: some people can remember a lot of things, some people only a few. She says that her working memory isn't always perfect, so she often does things to help it out. She shows Jon some cue cards that she made to help her when she gives a speech. Each cue card has a word and a picture, to remind her of all the things she wants to say in her speech. When she sees each cue, she remembers what to say next, just as Jon had remembered what to do in response to the cues in the game that they played.

The following weekend Jon has an assignment from his therapist. Chores are a sore point in their household. Mia has always been frustrated that she has to remind Jon each and every step of the way. Jon's assignment is to use the time-honored habit of making a list to supplement his working memory and free him from dependence on his mother's reminders. To engage Jon's interest and sense of fun, the therapist has given this tool a playful spin. It will be a "wrist list." Jon sits down at the table and cuts a piece of paper into strips. He then writes his chores on the strips, one chore per strip. Next, with Mia's help, he puts them in the order they are to be done. The final chore is his favorite–taking his dog to the park for a long walk. Finally, Jon puts the strips together to create a paper chain. Once the chain is completed, he attaches it to his wrist so that it will always be at " the point of performance" as he moves about completing his chores.

An hour later, chores done, Mia, Jon, and the dog are on their way to the park. "That was fun," Jon says to his mother. "And I got all my chores done by myself! Let's do that again next week."

Mia reflects that it doesn't matter whether Jon relies on his working memory or uses a list. The results are what she cares about. She is pleased that the chores got done but is even more pleased to see that Jon himself is so pleased. She was right; Jon is motivated to succeed. But she had been expecting him to succeed in ways that were not in line with his development. She sees now that, with the right external support, Jon can experience the success that he so much wants for himself.

References

Barkley, R. (2005). *ADHD and the Nature of Self-Control.* New York: The Guilford Press.

Zelazo. P.D. (July 29, 2005). Executive Function Part Four: Brain growth and the development of executive function. Aboutkidshealth.ca. Retrieved March 17, 2009, from http://www.aboutkidshealth.ca/news/Executive-Function-Part-Four-Brain-growth-and-the-development-of-executive-function.aspx?articleID=8071&categoryID=news-type

This article by Marcie Yeager, LCSW, RPT-S, was originally published as
Executive Function: A Key to Understanding the ADHD Mind
in the June 2009 issue of **Play Therapy** magazine.

The Simon Says Program:
Integrating EF into an ADHD Treatment Plan

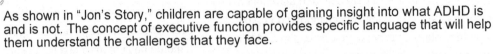

As shown in "Jon's Story," children are capable of gaining insight into what ADHD is and is not. The concept of executive function provides specific language that will help them understand the challenges that they face.

With the Simon Says program, using the "language of play," the therapist can:
1. Help the child understand the importance of skills/abilities related to executive function
2. Give the child opportunities to demonstrate behaviors related to executive function
3. help the child acquire habits and tools that will enable them to compensate for EF-related difficulties

The Simon Says program is intended to be one part of an overall treatment plan for ADHD.

It should, of course, be noted that there is currently no "cure" for ADHD and that all aspects of treatment are directed toward the successful *management* of this condition. Typically, this management includes:
• **medication**,
• **adaptations** in the school setting, and
• **behavior management** at home.

While these interventions are effective, the child is for the most part, a passive (and sometimes resistant) recipient of these interventions. The *Simon Says* program is meant to
• engage the child as an **active participant** in treatment by providing child-friendly **insight, tools and strategies.**

Skills learned in the Simon Says program prepare the child for long-term goals.

ADHD is a long-term condition, and management of this condition will need to continue over many years. Parents will need to be prepared to manage their child's treatment throughout their formative years. But many individuals diagnosed with ADHD continue to experience difficulties into their adult years. With the *Simon Says* program, our aim is to begin--in the elementary and middle school years--to instill in the child an accurate understanding of ADHD. With the right foundation, that child will grow into a young adult who has the insight and tools to thrive on his or her own.

Co-existing conditions and issues
It is important to keep in mind that ADHD doesn't exist in a vacuum.

First, some children diagnosed with ADHD have co-existing conditions, including Specific Learning Disabilities, Anxiety, Oppositional Defiant Disorder, and Conduct Disorder.
Second, many children referred for treatment for ADHD are also dealing with other life issues such as trauma and/or grief and loss.

While ADHD may be what brings the child to the therapist's office, it is also important for the therapist to identify and address these other conditions and issues.

How to Use the Simon Says Manual

This manual is divided into four sections, each focusing on a particular executive function:

Section 1: Working Memory
Section 2: Behavioral Inhibition
Section 3: Shifting Focus
Section 4: Goal Orientation

Each section provides ways for the therapist to provide **external support** for that function. This is done in two ways:

1. *Play activities* - Play is a natural way that children learn and practice behaviors that are essential to their development. For example, such games as *Mother May I*, *Simon Says*, and *Freeze Tag* require children to demonstrate **behavioral inhibition**. Play provides an engaging external framework for children to practice regulating their actions—over and over again. Children with ADHD, by the nature of the condition, internalize more slowly and therefore will benefit from increased opportunities to use the natural medium of **play** to support their developmental progression from external to internal regulation.

2. *Habits and tools* - Children with ADHD make slower progress in internalizing regulation of their thoughts and behavior. Studies show that even when these children become adults, some executive functions may be less developed. Many adults with ADHD learn to compensate by using tools that externalize the executive functions. We previously cited the simple example of using a list as an external aid to working memory. This tool, when used consistently, can help the person with poor working memory perform on the same level as a person with much better working memory. In this manual, stories and assignments introduce children to the concept of using tools that will help them to direct their behavior toward desired goals.

Order and Pace of Program

Order: It is recommended that the four sections of the program be used in the *order* outlined in the manual, as each of these sections (*Working Memory*, *Response Inhibition*, *Switching Focus*, and *Goal Orientation*) builds on information and tools presented in the previous section.

Pace: However, it is up to the therapist to determine the best pace at which to move through the program. There is great variance from one child to another as to how much time and repetition they need in order to incorporate the material into their daily lives.

The P.L.A.Y. Formula:
How It Works

Each section of the manual is divided into four steps:

Step 1: **P**lay

A playful activity introduces an executive function and allows the child to successfully perform actions related to that executive function.

Step 2: **L**ink

Stories give a child-friendly example of the importance of the executive function in real life. Worksheets link the function to everyday situations.

Step 3: **A**ssign

Several options for assignments are included in each section. These assignments give the child opportunities to practice behaviors related to the function and also provide tools to strengthen their performance in relation to that function.

Step 4: **Y**ahoo!

The final step provides ways for the therapist and coach to acknowledge effort and reinforce success.

STEP 1: **P**lay 	**What:** A playful activity introduces an executive function (or a group of functions) and allows the child to successfully perform actions related to that function.
	Who: Therapist leads the intervention for the child. (The child's family can be included.)
	Where: Therapist's office. (Families may like to have a copy of the activity to play at home.)
STEP 2: **L**ink 	**What:** A real-life story shows a child experiencing a problem in his or her daily activities. (In order to make the stories more interactive, they are written in "play" form so that–if desired–the child, family members, and therapist can role-play the story.) The story is followed by *Questions for Discussion* and *How Do People Use These Skills in Real Life?* worksheets. Each of these activities links the executive function to real life, real people. (Note: The therapist may need to make adaptations according to the child's reading and comprehension level.)
	Who: Therapist leads the intervention for the child. (The child's family can be included.)
	Where: Therapist's office. (Families may like to have a copy of the story to read at home.)
STEP 3: **A**ssign 	**What:** Several options for assignments are included in each section. These assignments give the child opportunities to practice behaviors related to the executive function and also provide tools to strengthen their performance in relation to that function.
	Who: Therapist selects the assignment, and makes sure child and coach understand and will be able carry out assignment. The coach oversees the implementation of the assignment in the child's daily life.
	Where: The assignments are carried out at home or in the classroom.
STEP 4: **Y**ahoo! 	**What**: Both the therapist and the parent/coach should acknowledge effort and reinforce success as the child carries out the assignments. Three reproducible pages are provided for the the therapist and parent to use: 1. *Encouraging Words:* This page gives examples of statements that the therapist and coach can make to point out areas of progress and to direct attention, in positive ways, to areas that still need some improvement. 2. *Skill Tracker:* This page that can be copied and given to other adults in the child's life. The skill-tracker gives them the opportunity to recognize–in writing–occasions when the child uses the information and self-help tools that are currently being targeted. 3. *Good Job! Tickets:* The therapist can copy these and award them to the child when reviewing assignments (and/or at other times as determined by the therapist). If desired, the tickets can later be exchanged for simple rewards at the therapist's office.
	Who: The therapist provides copies of the *Encouraging Words* page and the *Skill Trackers* for use in the child's daily life. The therapist decides how to use the *Yahoo!* Tickets and explains the process to the child.
	Where: *Encouraging Words* are examples of statements that can be used by the therapist in the office and by the coach outside of the office. *Skill Trackers* are used in the child's everyday environment. *Good Job!* Tickets are given at the therapist's office.

For the COACH:

What is Executive Function?

Executive functions are a collection of related, yet distinct, abilities that allow the growing child to begin to direct and regulate his or her own behavior.

Studies have demonstrated that these functions:
1) Are performed by the pre-frontal lobes of the cerebral cortex
2) Develop throughout childhood and into late adolescence
3) Allow for a shift from **outer** to **inner** control of behavior

Executive functions (EF) develop somewhat independently of general intelligence, talents, and skills. But EF is crucial to being able to reliably use one's intelligence, talents and skills in everyday life. As EF develops, the child is able to more and more consistently harness his abilities and steer them toward a particular end result.

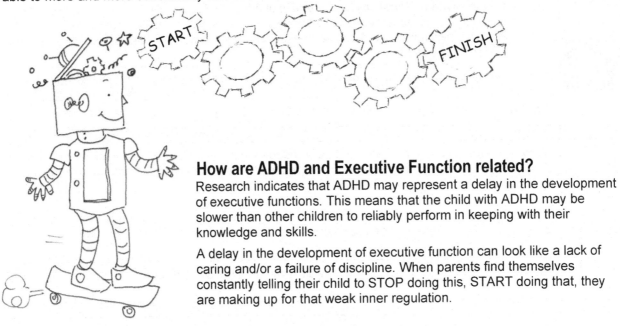

How are ADHD and Executive Function related?

Research indicates that ADHD may represent a delay in the development of executive functions. This means that the child with ADHD may be slower than other children to reliably perform in keeping with their knowledge and skills.

A delay in the development of executive function can look like a lack of caring and/or a failure of discipline. When parents find themselves constantly telling their child to STOP doing this, START doing that, they are making up for that weak inner regulation.

Why don't rewards and punishment work with my child?

Your child's need for reminders can be especially frustrating when siblings or classmates easily regulate their thoughts and actions, thus attaining rewards and avoiding punishments that are part of traditional discipline programs. It's very important to realize that failure of traditional discipline is neither your fault nor the child's.

Punishment and rewards come after the fact. Until your child's brain functioning matures, they will continue to need more external support "in the moment" in order to complete everyday tasks. But that doesn't mean that you have to provide all of the support by standing beside them every minute, directing them. Your child can learn strategies to help them compensate for their weak inner regulation.

What is the key to getting the best results?

It's important that those strategies be used at the **point of performance**–in the places and at the times that your child is having difficulty. In the **Simon Says** program, your role is that of "coach" to your child. Your child's therapist will educate your child about ADHD, suggest strategies, and recommend tools that they can use to help themselves. As your child's coach, you'll be in charge of helping your child use the strategies and tools at the **point of performance**–*when* and *where* they are needed in everyday life.

What ADHD is NOT:
ADHD does **not** mean your child is less intelligent, talented or skilled than other children.

What ADHD is:
ADHD is believed to be a **delay in** the development of the shift from outer to inner regulation of behavior. Expect children with ADHD to need more external support than other children in order to fully use their intelligence, talents and skills.

How the *Simon Says* Program Can Help Your Child

Executive Function	Example	Coach's Role	Strategies for Success*
Working Memory Holding information in mind in order to take the right action at the right time	Child is almost always late for the bus because he/she forgets to do all of the things needed to be ready for school.	*I can play games to help my child understand the concept of working memory.* *I can teach my child to use* **cues** *as a tool to provide external support for working memory. We can put our heads together and figure out what kind of cues will work best to "grab" my child's attention and help him/her remember to do the right thing at the right time.*	- Set up **cues** for times when my child needs external support for his/her working memory. - **Adjust the cues** as needed for my child. - Use a **series of cue**s for complex tasks, like getting ready for school.
Response Inhibition Stopping oneself from taking undesired actions	1. Child plays with the dog instead of getting dressed for school. 2. Child gets angry at someone and lashes out.	*Using play, I can help my child practice* **STOPPING** *in response to specific cues.* *Then, I can use the same cues to remind my child to stop himself/herself n "real-life" situations. I can teach my child the concept of* **on-track** *and* **off-track** *to help him/her set intentions and better understand goal*	- Create a visual "map" to help my child think ahead about ways to stay on-track and/or get back on track. - When my child gets off-track, **cues** can help my child remember his/her intentions and goals, stop unwanted actions, and get back on track.
Switching Focus Moving from one activity to another as the situation demands	Parent tells child to stop playing outside because it's time go to the store. Child doesn't want to switch and throws a fit.	*I can play games with my child that teach skills for calming down and "switching focus."* *With practice, these skills will become more habitual, and it will be easier for him/her to calm down and* **switch focus** *in real-life situations.*	- Practice doing a "cool-down" (specific strategies for relaxing, calming down, and changing focus.) - Use a STOP sign as a visual cue to help with self-calming.
Goal Orientation Establishing an image of a goal in one's mind and using that internal image to direct one's behavior.	Child is told to clean room before going outside to play ball. When friends arrive, child is in room, playing a game, and the room is still a mess.	*I can give my child a way to externalize a goal by helping him/her make a* **visual game plan.** *A game plan provides a concrete way to "see" what needs to be done. It also gives my child a way to keep* **track of his/her progress** *toward completion of a goal.*	- Help my child make a visual **game plan.** - Use fun activities to help my child be more aware of his/her ability to **sense passage of time.** - Introduce habit of using a timer to provide external support to inner sense of time.

* These strategies can help your child be more successful in every day life. And, since many children don't outgrow ADHD, those habits and tools can serve them for many years to come.

Hi! My Name Is Simon and I Have ADHD.

Before I learned what ADHD really is, I used to think maybe I was *just dumb*.

But I learned that people with ADHD are as smart as anyone else. But sometimes they have a problem doing the right thing at the right time

For example, they may:

#1 forget all about what they are supposed to be doing

#2 do something else instead

#3 have trouble stopping one thing in order to begin something else

#4 have trouble getting a big job started and then getting it finished on time

Some days, I have problems with all four of these things! See my examples on the next page...

I go to a therapist and I've learned that I don't have to get smarter. (*I'm already smart!*) I just have to understand the *reason* I am having difficulty, then learn some ways to help myself. And guess what? It's fun!

- We always start out by playing a game.

- Next, we read a story about another kid who is a lot like me.

- Then, I practice some stuff at home or school with my **coach**. (That's my mom or dad or teacher.)

I feel really happy and proud when we figure out good ways for me to help myself.

Here Are Some of the Things I Have Learned So Far:

Here's an example of what happens:	The *reason* it happens is because I have difficulty with:	My therapist teaches me things I can do to help myself. For example:
#1 When I get ready for school, I usually forget to do some of the things that I'm supposed to do. My parents fuss at me to do this, do that.	**Working Memory** I have trouble keeping things in my mind so I can take the right action at the right time.	*I use **cues** to help me remember to do the right thing at the right time.* *My therapist, coach and I put our heads together and figure out what kind of cues will grab my attention and be a good reminder of what to do.*
#2 I play with the dog instead of getting dressed for school. I get mad at my friend and do something mean instead of explaining what's wrong.	**Response Inhibition** It's hard for me to stop myself. Sometimes my brain doesn't even **realize** I'm doing the wrong thing until it's too late.	*I play games to practice stopping myself. In the games, when I get a **cue**, I have to stop what I'm doing and not move at all.* *Then, my coach uses those cues in real life to help me remember to stop myself.*
#3 My mom tells me to stop playing because it's time to go to the store. I don't want to do it and I throw a fit.	**Switching Focus** Once my brain is focused on one thing, it has a hard time letting go of that thing and focusing on something else.	*I've learned how to do a **cool-down**. I know how to breathe slowly and how to relax my whole body.* *The cool-down helps my brain and my body get ready to switch focus and do the right thing.*
#4 When it's time to clean my room, I have a hard time getting started. Even when I really **want** to get it done, I get distracted and don't get finished on time.	**Goal Orientation** I don't have a good picture in my mind of all the things I need to do and of how fast I need to work to get the job done.	*When I have a big job to do, I make a **game plan**. It's a picture on paper, so I can **see** all the things I need to do and which one to do first. It has a START and a FINISH, so it looks kind of like a game board. I even use a game marker to keep track of my progress so I can get the job done and feel proud.*

Simon Says

That's My Cue!

Help Kids Improve Their

Working Memory

SECTION 1: *That's My Cue!*
(Working Memory)

Rationale for *That's My Cue!* Activities

What is the problem?

Children with ADHD often fail to get things done at the right time and in the right way. Parents and teachers may describe them as distracted and forgetful: their attention wanders "all over the place." One parent describes a typical morning scene: "I wake him up and tell him to get dressed. When I come back to check, he is still daydreaming Then he is playing with the dog instead of eating breakfast, looking out the window instead of packing his book-sack. If I didn't *constantly* bring his attention back to the task at hand, he'd still be in his pajamas when the bus comes."

Often the adult has to raise their voice to get the child's attention (and perhaps even make threats to get the child to move in the right direction.) The child may apologize and promise to do better. But the very next time, it's the same thing all over again.

What executive functions are involved?

The executive functions involved are those of:
- *Working memory* (holding information in mind for the purpose of *completing* a task or activity).
- *Initiating* the required behavior (getting dressed, eating breakfast).

The demands of working memory are more complex when the task or activity involves a *series* of behaviors (dressing, eating, brushing teeth, *and* getting books ready.) For a child with mature working memory, it's no problem to recall and perform this sequence of events day after day. For the child with immature working memory, failure to develop these daily routines may make parents think that their child "just doesn't care. "

How can we provide external support for working memory?

Children can learn to **use cues as a tool** to help them remember to get things done in the right way and at the right time.

Cues provide **external support** for working memory, helping children remember to **initiate** the necessary behavior. A good cue is "sticky." It reaches out, grabs our attention, and reminds us clearly of what we need to do. (An even better cue reminds us *why* we need to do it.)

Parents can experiment to find cues that will be strong enough to "grab" the child's attention. Cues can be auditory, visual, or even tactile, and some children will benefit from multi-sensory cues. For more complex behaviors, a series of cues can help to prompt a series of tasks.

Remember: To be effective, cues need to be at the point of performance.

An important goal in this section is involving the child in thinking about how to set up a cue in such a way that the cue will effectively "grab" their attention at the *point of performance*: the moment in their day when they need to remember to initiate a particular action. For example, if the child makes a cue card as a reminder, they may need help in figuring out a good spot to post the cue card, where it won't be overlooked. If the first spot you try doesn't work, try others. Remember that the child's **effort to solve the problem** is the essential **first step** toward success. Give encouragement to keep on trying.

The child can also help make a cue card for a parent to use, and help the parent think about where to put it. Whether done for self or others, this activity is a good way to learn about the concept of using written reminders as cues, and placing them at the point of performance for maximum benefit.

Overview of *That's My Cue!* Activities

	Activity or Assignment	Purpose	Page
STEP 1: **P**lay	*Simon Says Pay Attention*	In this game, children listen to a story and demonstrate their ability to use their **working memory** and to **initiate** the "right" action in response to cues. This activity also introduces the idea of adapting cues to the child's needs.	20
STEP 2: **L**ink	**Story:** ***The Morning D.J.***	When Jen's father had to give a speech, he and Jen made "cue cards" to help him remember what to say. Now her father shows Jen how to use a sequence of auditory cues to aid her working memory and help her to initiate the tasks required in getting ready for school in the morning.	27
	Worksheets	A review of the importance of cues in everyday life.	30
STEP 3: **A**ssign	*Don't Forget!* **Cue Cards**	Child makes reminder cards to post at the "point of performance."	37
	Secret-Signal Cues	Child and coach collaborate to come up with signals that can serve as cues to remind child to initiate certain actions. The signals need to be strong enough to **grab** the child's attention.	41
	Wrist Lists	As with Jen in *The Morning D.J.* story, these lists provide sequential cues for a *series* of tasks. Because the cues are attached to the wrist, they are always at the **point of performance**!	43
	Ready, Set, *GO For It!*	This activity introduces the concept of working memory and gives the child and opportunity to "test" his/her working memory.	51
STEP 4: **Y**ahoo!	Encouraging Words Skill Tracker *Good Job!* Tickets	Adults provide feedback and encouragement as child tries new strategies and tools to improve working memory.	53

If you want to SUCCEED, here are the skills that you'll NEED!

Simon Says Pay Attention

❑   **Remember** what action to take

❑   Wait for your **cue**

❑   When you get your cue, **take the right action**

❑   If you have difficulty, **adjust the cue**

Play Intervention:
Simon Says Pay Attention

In the game outlined on the next three pages, children listen to a story and demonstrate their ability to use their **working memory** and to **initiate** the "right" action in response to cues. This activity also introduces the idea of *adjusting cues* to the child's needs.

Begin by giving the child a copy of the checklist on this page. The checklist explains what the child needs to do to succeed at playing *Simon Says Pay Attention*. Go over the checklist with the child *before* playing the game and use it again to review *after* playing the game.

The purpose of the game is to show children that they can already perform these skills in the context of play. In the steps following this **P**lay activity (**L**ink, **A**ssign, and **Y**ahoo!) the child and coach will learn strategies and tools that will help the child perform these skills in other contexts in day-to-day life.

If you want to SUCCEED, here are the skills that you'll NEED!

Simon Says Pay Attention

❑   **Remember** what action to take

❑   Wait for your **cue**

❑   When you get your cue, **take the right action**

❑   If you have difficulty, **adjust the cue**

If you want to SUCCEED, here are the skills that you'll NEED!

Simon Says Pay Attention

❑   **Remember** what action to take

❑   Wait for your **cue**

❑   When you get your cue, **take the right action**

❑   If you have difficulty, **adjust the cue**

 **Play**

Simon Says Pay Attention

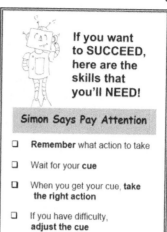

Materials:
You will need the story at the bottom of this page and a copy of the Skills Checklist on the previous page.

Get Ready:
Tell the child:
> The name of today's activity is **Simon Says Pay Attention.**

Show the child the Skills Checklist and read each item.
> Are you ready to succeed? Do you have the skills that you need? ...Let's get started!

Get Set:
Have the child stand at the opposite end of the room from you, about twelve steps away.
> I am going to read you a story. Every time you hear one of the "magic words", that is your **cue** to take one step forward. There are **four** magic words: **Simon ... Says ... Pay ... Attention.** Each time you hear any one of those words, take just one step forward. It can't be too big and it can't be too small. Let's practice.

Make adjustments if needed.
> Yes, you've got it. That's just the right size. You are going to take a step just that size when you hear one of the cue words, and **only** when you hear a cue word. If you take a step when you haven't heard the cue word or if you don't take a step at all, or if you take the wrong-size step, you have to go back and start again! So **listen for your cue**, and take the right action at just the right time. Are you ready to begin?

Go:
Read the story–slowly. Observe whether or not the child responds to each of the cues, but do not provide any help if the child misses a cue. That will be the next part of this activity.

Far away, up on a hill, there lives a little rabbit. His name is **Simon.**

Every morning, **Simon** wakes up and **says** good morning to the world. Then he starts to explore, going up and down the hill, back and forth, moving to the right and then to the left. He sniffs around, looking for something to eat. He doesn't have to go to the store and **pay** for his food like we do. It's all right there for him to take. Whatever comes to his **attention**, that looks good, **Simon** eats it right up. This morning, **Simon** doesn't eat everything that he finds. So, there is some left for the other rabbits. But he doesn't leave much, so they will have to **pay** close **attention**. "I'll come back later to see if they found it," **Simon says** to himself.

Review: In this activity, the player has to utilize his/her *working memory* in order to respond to a *verbal cue*. First, use the skills checklist, and point out what the player did correctly:

You used your working memory to remember what action to take (just one step, etc.).

Continue through the checklist
Note: There are eleven cues in the preceding story.

1. If the child responded to all or most of the eleven cues without help, go through all of the items on the checklist. Then raise the level of challenge by going on to the next activity. (Simon Says Pay Attention #2, page 23.)

2. However, if the player had some difficulty responding to all of the cues, tell the player:

Remember that one of the skills on the checklist was **"If you have difficulty, adjust the cue."** *Let's think about ways to make the cues easier to pay attention to.*

In order to understand why the child had difficulty, ask questions such as:

What made it sometimes difficult to respond to a cue?
What did you do to help yourself when it was difficult?
What can I do to help you respond to the cues?

If you want to SUCCEED, here are the skills that you'll NEED!

Simon Says Pay Attention

☐ **Remember** what action to take

☐ Wait for your **cue**

☐ When you get your cue, **take the right action**

☐ If you have difficulty, **adjust the cue**

Possible ways to modify cues to provide more external support:

- Strengthen the verbal cue by changing the tone or volume of voice.
- Strengthen the verbal cue by adding eye contact.
- Pair the verbal cue with another type of cue: visual or tactile.
- Write the cue words on a piece of paper for the child to look at as the story is read.
- Have an additional "private cue" to serve as a signal that a cue has been missed.

Be creative in finding cues that will work for the child!

Play It Again: With the child, decide how to "adjust the cue" and then repeat the activity, giving enough support so that the child responds to all eleven of the cues. It's OK to stop in the middle and make further modifications to strengthen the cues, if needed.

When finished, go over the checklist and talk about the skills that the child demonstrated.

Simon Says Pay Attention #2

(Use after player has shown mastery at the previous activity.)

Review: You can make the *Simon Says Pay Attention* activity more challenging by following the directions below. But it is very tricky. Have fun and don't take it too seriously! It might be a good idea to have the parent do this along with the child.

Tell the child:

*Are you ready to try again, and make it a whole lot harder? This time, you will take different actions for different cues. You will still take one step forward when you hear the cue words **Simon** and **Says** and **Pays** and **Attention**. But if you hear the word **Back**, that's your cue to move one step back. And if you hear the word **Right**, that's your cue to move one step to the right. And if you hear the word **Left**, that's your cue to move one step to the left. Remember the skills: you not only have to listen carefully for the cues, you have to take the right action at the right time and **only** at the right time. Are you ready?*

Far away, up on a hill, there lives a little rabbit. His name is **Simon.**

Every morning **Simon** wakes up and **says** good morning to the world. Then he starts to explore, going up and down the hill, <u>back</u> and forth, moving to the <u>right</u> and then to the <u>left</u>. He sniffs around, looking for something to eat. He doesn't have to go to the store and **pay** for his food like we do. It's all <u>right</u> there for him to take. Whatever comes to his **attention** that looks good, **Simon** eats it <u>right</u> up. This morning, **Simon** doesn't eat everything that he finds. So, there is some <u>left</u> for the other rabbits. But he doesn't leave much, so they will have to **pay** close **attention**. "I'll come <u>back</u> later to see if they found it," **Simon says** to himself.

After **Simon** eats, he turns his **attention** to other things. "I think I will go <u>back</u> up the hill and **pay** my respects to Mrs. Robin," he **says.** And **Simon** hops <u>right</u> over to the tree where she lives. "Hi there, **Simon**," **says** Mrs. Robin, peering over the edge of her nest. "Let me finish feeding my babies, and then I will give you my full **attention."** She turns <u>back</u> to her babies and feeds them until there isn't a worm <u>left</u>. Then she turns <u>back</u> to **Simon**. "I'll be <u>right</u> with you as soon as I get them all tucked in." She tucks each baby into the nest. She gives special **attention** to the little one, who wiggles a lot and sometimes falls <u>right</u> out of the nest. Then she turns <u>back</u> to **Simon** and flies down to meet him. "Hi, **Simon**," she **says**. "I'm so glad you've come to **pay** me a visit."

23

Review: In this activity, the player has to utilize his/her working memory in order to respond to a verbal cue. First, point out what the player did correctly:

> *You used your working memory to know what action to take (one baby step forward or back or right or left.) When your heard the cue, you took the correct action.*

If the player had some difficulty responding to all of the cues, tell the player:

> *Remember that one of the skills on the checklist was* **"If you have difficulty, adjust the cue."** *Let's think about ways to make sure that the cues really grab your attention.*

Some questions to ask:

> *What made it sometimes difficult to respond to the cues?*
> *What did you do to help yourself when it was difficult?*
> *What can I do to help you respond to the cues?*
> *What can we do to make sure the cues really grab your attention?*

Play It Again: With the child, decide how to "adjust the cue" and then repeat the activity, giving enough support so that the child responds to all eleven of the cues. It's OK to stop in the middle and make further modifications to strengthen the cues, if needed.

When finished,
review the checklist
and
give a big *Yahoo!*

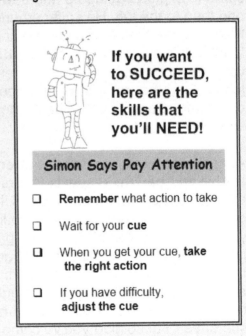

If you want to SUCCEED, here are the skills that you'll NEED!

Simon Says Pay Attention

❑ **Remember** what action to take

❑ Wait for your **cue**

❑ When you get your cue, **take the right action**

❑ If you have difficulty, **adjust the cue**

COACHING TIP   This section is all about using cues as reminders to help the child do the right thing at the right time. The first step, of course, is to have the child declare their intention to succeed by responding to an agreed-upon cue. Then, to be effective as reminder, cues have to stand out from the background of everything else that is going on (both external and internal) and "grab" the child's attention.

As you continue with the activities in this section, remember that if at first a cue is not successful, tweak it and try again. Verbal cues can be modified by adding eye contact or a gentle touch, and by varying the tone or volume of voice. (Sometimes a whispered cue is more effective than a loud one!) Visual cues can be varied in many different ways: be creative! You'll discover lots of ideas in the pages ahead.

COACHING TIP

Make this story come alive!

The story on the next page is written so that it can be read aloud as a "play."

There are four parts in this story. They are:
1) Mother
2) Narrator
3) Jen
4) Father

To make the parts easier to read, make a copy of the story for each reader. On each copy, highlight the part(s) to be performed by that reader.

Have fun!

When do people use these skills in Real Life?

When Jen's father had to give a speech, he and Jen made "cue cards" to help him remember what to say.

When Jen has difficulty getting ready for school in the morning, her father shows her how to use cues to help her remember to do the right thing at the right time.

The Morning D.J.

Mother: Jen? Jen! Are you still in bed? ... You'll be late for school again! Get going. You need to make your bed, eat your breakfast, brush your teeth, comb your hair, get dressed, check your book sack, and be outside to meet the bus at 7:30 sharp.

Narrator: Jen sighed. She wished it was still summer. She made her bed and went to the kitchen for breakfast. Waffles! Her favorite! She felt a little better.

She sat down to eat her waffles. Uh-oh! The dog dish was empty. That was Jen's job. She got up and put out fresh food and water. Ginger came up and licked her hand.

Jen: Hi Ginger.

Narrator: Jen petted her soft fur. Ginger ran under the kitchen table and brought out a tennis ball.

Jen: OK Ginger, I'll play ball with you.

Narrator: She opened the back door and the two of them ran outside. Soon Jen was laughing and having a good time.

Father: Jen! What are you *doing?*... You're still in your pajamas. The bus will be here in 15 minutes!

Jen: I'm sorry. Ginger wanted to play ball, and I....

Father: I don't want to hear it! We can't go another year with you missing the bus. Get going. And I mean *now!*

....

Narrator: At dinner that night, Jen's parents said they wanted to talk with her.

Mother: Honey, your father and I have been talking. We love you and we don't like yelling at you to get ready every morning.

Narrator: Jen looked at her mom and almost started to cry. She *hated* being yelled at.

Jen: I'm trying. I don't know what happens. I guess I just forget what I'm supposed to be doing.

Father: Yes, I think that is exactly the problem. And I heard about an idea that we think will help you remember what it is you are supposed to be doing.

Narrator: Jen looked at her dad, wondering what he was going to say next.

Father: Remember when you helped me make the cue cards for my speech?

PAGE 2

Narrator: Jen's dad had to make a speech at a meeting. He was worried that he might forget some of the things he was supposed to say. So he made a set of *cue cards*. On each card, he put a word that would be a *cue*–a *reminder*–of what to say next. Then Jen drew a picture for each card, as an extra *cue*.

Father: Those cue cards helped me a lot. Without those cues, I would have forgotten some of the things I was supposed to say at the meeting, just like you forget some of the things you are supposed to do in the morning.

Jen: That was fun making cue cards! I liked drawing the pictures to help you remember what to say!

Father: Well, this new idea will be fun, too. It's called *The Morning D.J.* But instead of *seeing* your cues on cards you'll *hear* your cues–we'll put them on your iPod.

Jen: A *D.J.* like on the radio?

Father: Exactly! Here's the idea: You'll pretend that you are a D.J., and you'll choose some songs and put them on your iPod. The songs will be the *cues* to remind you what to do. No one will have to fuss at you!

Jen: How can songs be cues?

Father: You'll choose a song for each thing that you need to do in the morning. For example, you'll choose one song to listen to while you make your bed. When that song *starts,* you know it's time to make your bed–and you have to *finish* before the song is over.

Jen: I can do that!

Father: I know you can. And there will be a special song for each thing that you have to do in the morning. Each *song* will remind you of what task to do next. And you'll know that you have to get each task done before that song is over. That will help you get everything done on time.

Jen: I like that idea! Let's see, I have to make my bed, get dressed, eat, comb my hair, and brush my teeth… Oh, and feed Ginger! That's important. I love Ginger!

Mother: I know you do, and if you finish everything on time, you will still have plenty of time to play with Ginger or maybe even to watch TV.

Narrator: Jen smiled. She liked the sound of that. She hardly ever got to watch TV on school mornings.

Jen: When can I put the songs on my iPod?

Mother: As soon as we get the table cleared and the dishes washed.

Jen: Let's go. I'll be thinking of which songs I want while we work.

THE END

** The **Morning D.J.** technique was taken from the ADHD: Organizational Tips Section of About.com
(http://add.about.com/cs/organizationtips)

The Morning D.J.
Questions for Discussion

1. How do you think Jen feels about getting up in the morning for school?

2. How many things does Jen need to do to be ready for school? How many things do you need to do?

3. Was Jen being forgetful on purpose? (Explain your answer.)

4. Jen's parents could have punished her for not being ready. But they decided to try a new idea. How do you think Jen felt about that?

Extra Questions

Remember the skills that you needed to succeed when you played *Simon Says Pay Attention*. (see checklist at right) Which of those skills will Jen need to use to get ready in the morning using **The Morning D.J.**?

Working memory means that you can remember what it is that you need to do. Jen's father used cue cards to help his working memory. Jen is going to use songs as cues to help her working memory. When does *your* working memory need some help?

If you want to SUCCEED, here are the skills that you'll NEED!

Simon Says Pay Attention

☐ **Remember** what action to take

☐ Wait for your **cue**

☐ When you get your cue, **take the right action**

☐ If you have difficulty, **adjust the cue**

When using cues to aid working memory, remember that if the cues you select don't work, they can be adjusted or strengthened to be better "attention grabbers." For example, when Jen's father made his cue cards, she added a picture to his written words, thus *strengthening* the visual cue.

Note: The auditory cues in "The "Morning D.J." technique will serve a dual purpose:
1) Cueing Jen as to which task to **initiate** next and
2) Externalizing Jen's **sense of time**, as the length of each song will also guide her to complete the task within a specified time period.

If you want to SUCCEED, here are the skills that you'll NEED!

Simon Says Pay Attention

❑ **Remember** what action to take

❑ Wait for your **cue**

❑ When you get your cue, **take the right action**

❑ If you have difficulty, **adjust the cue**

When do people use these skills in Real Life?

Person	What's their cue? Choose one from "Cue" column	What is the right action to take? What happens if they take the right action?	What happens if they don't take the right action?	CUE
Person waiting at home for a friend to come for a visit				**A** Buzzing of alarm clock
Person swimming in the ocean				**B** **Ready, Set, *Go!***
Football player				**C** Lifeguard's whistle
Hot and hungry child with money to spend				**D** *Hike!*
Person sleeping in bed				**E** *Knock, Knock!*
Runner at the race starting line				**F** Music from ice cream truck

If you want to SUCCEED, here are the skills that you'll NEED!

Simon Says Pay Attention

☐ **Remember** what action to take

☐ Wait for your **cue**

☐ When you get your cue, **take the right action**

☐ If you have difficulty, **adjust the cue**

Link

When do people use these skills in Real Life?

How about <u>YOU</u>?

When do you need to use these skills in Real Life?

At SCHOOL, what are some cues that you should respond to?

1) _____ 2) _____

What action do you need to take?

1) _____ 2) _____

At HOME, what are some cues that you should respond to?

1) _____ 2) _____

What action do you need to take?

1) _____ 2) _____

With FRIENDS, what are some cues that you should respond to?

1) _____ 2) _____

What action do you need to take?

1) _____ 2) _____

Point of Performance and the Coach's Role

Because of the importance of using interventions at the **point of performance**, the role of the "coach" is an integral part of the *Simon Says Pay Attention* program. At home, a parent or other adult can act as coach. In a school setting, a teacher or other staff member can act as coach at the point of performance.

Using the Coach's Report

It is important to have good communication between the therapist and the coach, so that therapist can make adjustments to the program based on the particular needs of the child and the family (and/or classroom). The coach's report on the next page provides a concise way to keep the therapist and coach "on the same page" as the child progresses through the Simon Says program.

- We recommend that the therapist introduce the use of the **Coach's Report** during the **Link** activities and continue to use the reports as part of the **Assign** activities.
- The therapist can help the child and coach formulate goals during the therapy session, writing them directly on the **Coach's Report.**
- The **Coach's Report** can then go home with the coach at the end of each session.
- At the next session, the coach returns the completed form to the therapist prior to the start of the session.
- In addition to showing the progress the child has made on the goals, the report will update the therapist on any significant events that have occurred since the last session and any special concerns that need to be addressed.

The **Coach's Report** on the opposite page is specific for Section 1 of the Simon Says program. Use the *That's My Cue!* checklist to help formulate goals that are related to **working memory.**

Begin with simple goals. For example, after completing the Play and Link activities, possible goals might be:

Goal: Play "Simon Says Pay Attention" at home.

Goal: Notice cues in everyday life.

These goals get families used to thinking about working memory on a daily basis, and give them an opportunity to have some simple, interactive fun together.

For setting more complicated goals, see *Strategies for Success,* page 52.

COACH'S REPORT   Date_____

Child's Name _____

Coach's Name _____

1) Please list any significant events that have occurred since your child's last therapy session:

....
....
....
....

2) Brief description your child's behavior, mood, etc in the past week:

....
....
....

3) Do you have any specific concerns or questions today?

....
....
....

4) Progress toward goals

Goal: _____

Very Dissatisfied -2	Dissatisfied -1	Neutral - Unsure 0	Satisfied 1	Very Satisfied 2

Goal: _____

Very Dissatisfied -2	Dissatisfied -1	Neutral - Unsure 0	Satisfied 1	Very Satisfied 2

Goal: _____

Very Dissatisfied -2	Dissatisfied -1	Neutral - Unsure 0	Satisfied 1	Very Satisfied 2

Comments on goals:

....
....
....

Things to Do:

Name: _____

Date: _____

f you want
o SUCCEED,
iere are the
skills that
/ou'll NEED!

Simon Says Pay Attention

☐ **Remember** what action to take

☐ Wait for your **cue**

☐ When you get your cue, **take the right action**

☐ If you have difficulty, **adjust the cue**

REMEMBER:

You've got the skills that you need to succeed!

Assign

Assignment Idea # 1

Don't Forget! Cue Cards

Creating written reminders can be an effective way of providing oneself with a **cue** to take a particular action. And, the closer the reminder is to the **point of performance,** the more effective it will be.

Page 37

Assignment Idea # 2

Secret-Signal Cues

In Assignment #1, cue cards at the "point of performance" are used to help someone remember to initiate a particular action. This is a good technique when one can plan ahead and foresee the need for a reminder at a particular time and place. There are many times, however, when a child might need to be reminded to initiate an action in unplanned situations. To help in these circumstances, the parent and child can collaborate ahead of time and agree on "signals" that will cue the child to initiate a particular action.

Page 41

Assignment Idea # 3

Wrist Lists

Like Jen in the story, *The Morning D.J.*, many children have problems following through on all the steps involved in a particular activity or chore. Often parents find they must give reminders "every step of the way" in order for the child to complete the expected actions For people of all ages, **a list** is an excellent way to remind *oneself* of the next step, and to make sure that all steps are completed.

Page 43

Assignment Idea # 4

Ready, Set, *GO for It!*

Not everyone is blessed with a good **working memory**. It is important to understand the limits of one's ability to work from memory. With that understanding, we can either 1) use practice to improve our working memory or 2) find ways to give our memories a boost or a reminder by using **cues** or **lists** or other tools as *memory helpers.*

Page 51

 Use the **Things to Do** list to give the child a written reminder of the assignment.

COACHING TIP

Clapboards can be purchased from party supply stores and make a fun prop to teach children about working memory and initiating the right action at the right time. Explain that the *visual* cue of the clapboard and the *verbal* cue *"Lights, Camera, Action!"* are used by filmmakers to let everyone know that it is time to begin shooting a scene for a movie. Everyone has a job to do and the **cues** let each person know that it is time to begin doing their jobs.

In the home or in the classroom, cues can also be helpful in reminding people to take certain actions. This assignment provides visual cues (cards) but, if needed, the child may also benefit from a verbal cue from the coach.

And remember: *It's OK to measure success one small step at a time!*

Assign

Assignment Idea #1:
Don't Forget! Cue Cards

Executive Functions
- Working Memory
- Initiating Actions

RATIONALE: Creating written reminders can be an effective way of providing oneself with a **cue** to take a particular action. And, the closer the reminder is to the **point of performance,** the more effective it will be. (Point of performance means the time and place where you have to take that action.)

BENEFIT: This assignment can help the child acquire the helpful habit of using visual cues as **reminders** of things to do *and* thinking about the best placement for the reminders.

MATERIALS NEEDED: Copy the *Don't Forget!* **Cue Cards** (on the following page) on heavy paper. (**Hint**: To make it a better "attention grabber," create copies on brightly colored paper.)

EXPLANATION FOR CHILD:

Have you–or your parent–ever said, "Oh no, I completely forgot to _____
            (Fill in the blank: bring home my book, go to the bank, pick up the clothes from the cleaner)
Most people have, some more often than others! If you often forget, or if the thing to be done is very important, it's a good idea to write yourself a reminder. **That's the first step.**

The second step *is to think about the best place to put the reminder, so you'll be sure to see it at the right time.*

For example:

Where would be a good place to put each of these cue cards?

ASSIGNMENT:

Take home the **Don't Forget!** **Cue Cards** *and use them as cues to remind you "to do the right thing at the right time."*
1. *Write on the cue card the thing that you need to do.*
2. *Then think of the best place to put the card so you'll see it when and where you need to do that thing.*

Copy on heavy paper and cut to create four cue cards.

Copy on heavy paper and cut to create four cue cards.
Suggestion: If possible, copy on brightly colored paper!

39

COACHING TIP

Secret Signals Lead to Success!

A story about Olympic swimmer Michael Phelps, as cited in the April/May 2007 issue of *ADDitude Magazine*, can provide inspiration for teaching children about the use of cues. According to Michael's mother, Debbie Phelps, Michael was diagnosed with ADHD at age nine. She recalls a swim meet in which he came in second and angrily ripped off his goggles and threw them on the floor. She decided to teach him that good sportsmanship–and keeping one's composure–is as important as winning. Together, they came up with a signal that she could give him from the stands: she would form a "C" with her hand, which stood for "compose yourself."

Michael's mother knew that the plan was not only effective, but had "sunk in," when Michael gave her the "C" signal when she was getting stressed while making dinner.

- *"How to Raise a Superstar"* (2007)

Assignment Idea #2:
Secret-Signal Cues

Executive Functions
- Working Memory
- Initiating Actions

RATIONALE: In Assignment #1, cue cards at the **point of performance** are used to help someone remember to initiate a particular action. This is a good technique when one can plan ahead and foresee the need for a reminder at a particular time and place. There are many times, however, when a child might need to be reminded to initiate an action in unplanned situations. To help in these circumstances, the parent and child can collaborate ahead of time and agree on **signals** that will cue the child to initiate a particular action at the time and place needed.

BENEFIT: This assignment provides another step in helping the child think about how they can set up cues in their environment to help them do the right thing at the right time.

MATERIALS NEEDED: None

EXPLANATION FOR CHILD:

*We can't always plan ahead and use a **cue card** to remind us about what we need to do. But cards aren't the only kind of reminders that we can use. We can give one another **signals** that remind us to do something. We can even use **secret signals** for cues.*

> **Note**: If the child knows about Olympic swimmer Michael Phelps, tell the child the story of the cue that he and his mother developed when he was a child. (See opposite page.)

We all forget what to do sometimes, and secret signal cues can help us remember to do the right thing at the right time.

ASSIGNMENT:

The parent and child identify an action that the child sometimes forgets to take. Then they work out a signal that can be used to cue the child to take that action. As always in working with cues, if the cue doesn't work the first time, think of ways to adjust the cue to make it more effective.

Examples: Come up with a secret signal to cue the child to:
- Use *Please* and *Thank You*
- Shake hands
- Use your inside voice
- Put away your tennis shoes
- Go back and close the door
- Clear your plate

MOTIVATING: In the following assignment, **wrist lists** are used for those situations in which the child must take not just one action, but a series of actions. In order to provide additional motivation for the child to move through the series of tasks, the coach can also specify a special activity that will happen only after the child completes all of the tasks.

COACHING TIP

Keep this simple! Some possibilities for the special activity are:
- Reading a story or playing a short game
- Placing star on a chart that can be redeemed for a privilege at a later time
- Playing a computer game
- Sharing a snack

Each of the three wrist lists in the following assignment has a built-in way to include this "special activity."
1. With the *paper-chain list,* the activity can be written inside the wrist band.
2. With the *sticky list*, several icons (*Yahoo! Mission accomplished!*) are included that represent the child's success in completing the tasks. This final icon can be moved to signify that it is now time for the special activity.
3. With the *wrist checklist*, the special activity can be written on the last line, or written in the speech bubble at the bottom of the list.

FOLLOWING THROUGH:
The coach can also challenge the child to use the wrist list for three weeks, then see if they can use their **"working memory"** to complete the tasks after that.

But if they can't, that's OK. Provide external support for working memory as long as it is needed!

Assignment Idea #3:
Wrist Lists

Executive Functions
- Working Memory
- Initiating Actions

RATIONALE: Like Jen in the story, *The Morning DJ*, many children have problems following through on *all of the steps* involved in a particular activity or chore. Often parents find they must give reminders "every step of the way" in order for the child to complete the expected actions. While Jen's cues were *auditory*, a more traditional type of reminder is *visual*: a to-do list.

BENEFIT: The to-do lists in this assignment are "wrist lists" (as described in Jon's Story, pages 4-7). The wrist list engages the child's attention and—by virtue of being attached to the child's wrist—ensures that the list is always at the all-important **point of performance**.

MATERIALS NEEDED: See the individual instructions for materials needed.

Wrist List #1:
Paper-Chain Wrist List
Page 44

Wrist List #2:
Sticky Wrist List
Page 46

Wrist List #3
Wrist Checklist
Page 48

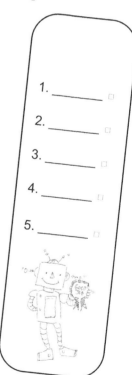

EXPLANATION FOR CHILD:
*In the story, **The Morning D.J.**, Jen had to remember to do a lot of things! One way to help yourself when you have to do a lot of things is to use a list. A list can help you remember all of the things you need to do. You are going to use a special kind of list called a **wrist list**. It will be attached to your wrist, so it will be easy to keep the list with you.*

COACH'S ROLE: The coach should choose a situation in which the child has difficulty following through on a job or activity. (Example: cleaning up toys or room.) The coach breaks the job down into five (or less) smaller steps and incorporates the steps into one of the wrist lists.

Wrist List #1: Paper-Chain Wrist List

MATERIALS NEEDED:
Copy the form on the next page to create:
  1. **Paper wrist band**
  2. **Paper strips** (which will form links for a paper chain.)

HOW TO MAKE THE PAPER-CHAIN WRIST LIST:

1. Copy the form on the next page.

2. Make the wristband. Write final (reward) activity on the wristband. Cut out and then fold in on dotted lines to hide the writing. (You will later wrap the wristband around child's wrist and tape the end.)

SAMPLE
(use form on next page)

wristband

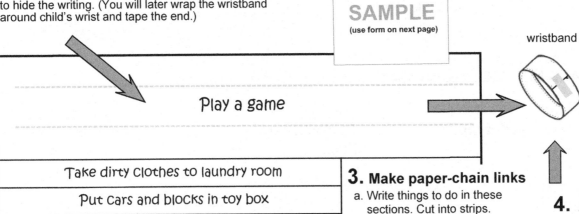

Play a game

Take dirty clothes to laundry room

Put cars and blocks in toy box

Put games on shelf

Take books to living room

Make bed

3. Make paper-chain links
  a. Write things to do in these sections. Cut into strips.
  b. Beginning with the first item to be done, bend strip into a circle and close with tape.
  c. Join the next circle to that one to create a chain.
  d. End with the last item to be done.

4. Attach
When you are ready for the child to begin, you will attach the chain to the wrist band. (The first thing to be done should be at the loose end.)

SUGGESTIONS FOR USING THE *PAPER-CHAIN WRIST LIST:*

1. On the wrist band, write the final (*reward*) activity and attach to the child's wrist. (To add suspense, keep the reward activity hidden from the child until the end of the assignment.)

2. Create the paper-chain list. Write the tasks to be done on the strips. Put them in the order to be done. (You may want to involve the child in the process of thinking about the best order for the tasks to be done.)

3. Attach the paper-chain to the child's wrist band, with the first item to be done at the loose end.

4. The child then removes the first link and does the task.

5. After completing that task, the child checks with the coach and removes the next link.

6. After all the links have been removed and all tasks have been completed, the child takes the wrist band to the coach and learns what the final activity is.

COPY this page and CUT on solid lines

Wristband: Write final (reward) activity here. Then fold in on dotted lines to hide the writing and keep it secret.

Links: Cut into strips. Write one task to be done on each strip. *Beginning with the first* item to be done, bend each strip into a circle and close with tape. Join the next strip to that one to create a chain.

End with the last task to be done, and attach that one to the wristband.

Wrist List #2: Sticky Wrist List

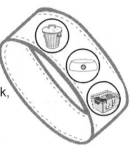

For jobs that need to be done on a daily basis, such as getting ready for school in the morning, or getting ready for bed at night, a **Sticky Wrist List** provides a re-usable alternative to the paper-chain wrist list. In this version, as the child completes each task, an icon is moved from the left (Action!) wrist band to the right (Yahoo!) wrist band.

MATERIALS NEEDED:

1) Copy the facing page on heavy paper.
2) Round Velcro™ tabs can be purchased at hobby and craft stores. You will need **12 sets** to complete the wrist lists as described below. (Each set contains two parts, a "fuzzy" tab and a "hook" tab.)

INSTRUCTIONS:

1. *For the wrist bands:*

- Cut out both bands.
- Laminate the wrist bands (you can use clear packaging tape if you don't have a laminator)
- Place them with the front side facing you.
- Place the Velcro™ tabs on the bands as follows:
   a. Note the **Checklist** and the **Thumbs-Up** icons at the *top* of the bands. Turn the bands over and put a **"fuzzy"** tab on the opposite side (behind the two icons.)
   b. Turn the bands so the front is facing you again. On each of the five colored spots, attach a **"hook"** tab.
   c. The last spot (with arrow) also receives a "hook" tab. This last tab will attach to the "fuzzy" tab that you put on the opposite side of the band, forming a closure for the band. Adjust the placement of the last "hook" tab to fit the child's wrist.

2. *For the "action" icons:*

- Choose ten of the icons (or create your own) to represent tasks/actions.
- Laminate the icons.
- Then attach the remaining ten "fuzzy" tabs to the back of each icon.

How to use the *Sticky Wrist List:*

1. The **Go!** band goes on the child's left wrist; the **Yahoo!** band goes on the child's right wrist.

2. Choose five icons representing actions to be taken.

3. Attach them to the tabs on the **Go!** wristband. (Put them in the order they should be completed, starting with the first tab under the **Go!** icon.)

4. The child then performs the first action (the one immediately under the **Go!** Icon.)

5. After completing that task, the child moves that icon to the **Yahoo!** band.

6. Continue to complete the actions represented by each icon, moving the icon from the left to the right wrist when it is completed.

7. The Yahoo! (Simon) icon can be used to represent a reward activity.

COACHING TIP

Sticky Wrist-List Variation

Here is a quicker and simpler alternative to using the laminated bands and **Velcro™** tabs:

1. Take two pieces of scotch tape or masking tape and wrap one around each of the child's wrist *with the sticky side facing out*.

2. Then just stick the (laminated) icons to the tape and move the icons from the left wrist to the right wrist as the items are completed.

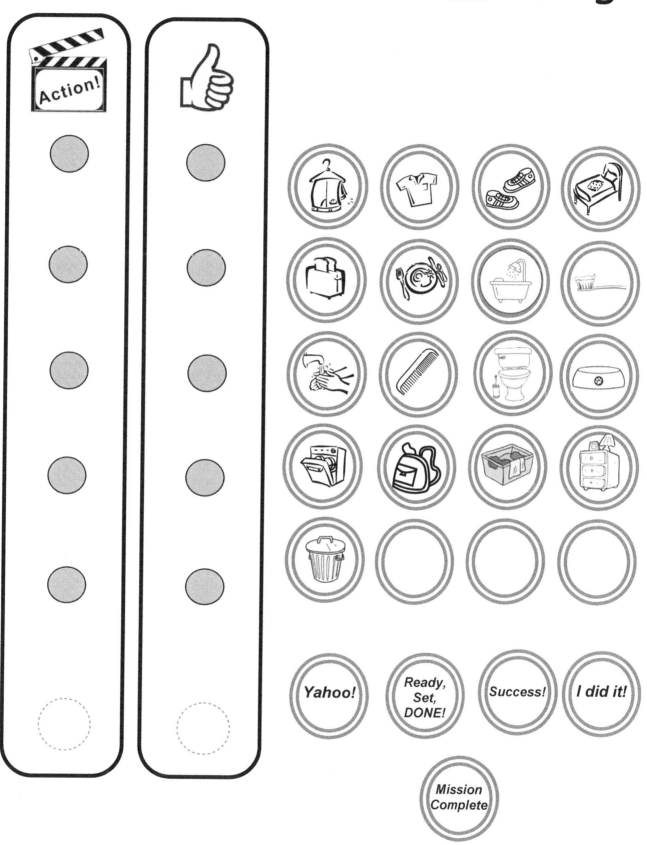

Action!

👍

Yahoo!

Ready, Set, DONE!

Success!

I did it!

Mission Complete

Wrist List #3: Wrist Checklist

This wrist list is the simplest. It is a basic "To-Do" list, the kind many people use every day, with two additions:
   1) It is attached to the wrist, so it is always at the **point of performance**.
   2) It includes a built-in motivator: the last item is something that the child wants to do (play a game, go outside, have a snack, watch TV, read a book). Encouraging words can also be written in the speech bubble.

Materials Needed:
Copy and cut out one of the wrist lists on the next page.

How to use the *Wrist Checklist:*

1. On the list, the coach writes down the tasks to be done, breaking them down into no more than five small steps. (The final item on the list can be a "reward" activity.)

2. Circle the list around the child's wrist and tape the ends together, with the list facing out.

3. The child completes the assigned tasks in the order on the list. After the child completes all of the items, remove the list. The child and coach should then go over the list together, placing a check by each item successfully completed.

4. If all items are checked, the child is allowed to do the final activity.

Alternate uses: The use of a checklist is an excellent habit for children to acquire early in life. Look for a variety of opportunities to use the wrist checklist. The more the child practices its use, in different situations, the better.

Some ideas for using the wrist checklist are:

• Have the child run errands with the parent, and assign the child the job of writing the checklist and reading it to he parent as they progress through the errands. Make the last item something fun–a stop at the park, a visit at grandma's.

• Have "chore day" at home and use wrist checklists to divide up the chores–one wrist list for each person. Make the final activity a family get-together. (For example, make some popcorn and play a game together.)

• Use the wrist checklist for planning and executing the steps for a fun activity such as getting ready for a party or family movie night.

The Power of the Humble Checklist!

If you read some of the many books, articles and websites offering advice to adults with ADHD, you will find that using a humble checklist is one of the top suggestions. There's a reason for this: as simple as they are, checklists work!

Research backs this up. A study at hospitals in Michigan found that enforcing a five-step checklist of anti-infection measures cut the infection rate at intensive care units by 66%. They estimated that over a period of 18 months, the use of the checklist saved many lives and millions of dollars.*

* A Life Saving Checklist (2007)

Assign

1. _____ ☐
2. _____ ☐
3. _____ ☐
4. _____ ☐
5. _____ ☐

1. _____ ☐
2. _____ ☐
3. _____ ☐
4. _____ ☐
5. _____ ☐

1. _____ ☐
2. _____ ☐
3. _____ ☐
4. _____ ☐
5. _____ ☐

COACHING TIP

The ***Ready, Set, Go!*** assignment helps the child understand the concept of **working memory**. Keep this activity FUN! Stop long before your child tires of it. Practice frequently, but for short periods of time.

Variation: Another game that involves working memory is ***We're Going on a Trip.***
1. The first player says:
> ***We are going on a trip and we're taking _____.***
(Player names an item to bring on the trip.)

2. The next person says:
> ***We are going on a trip and we're taking _____ and _____.***
(Player has to say the item named by the first person *and* add another item.)

3. Keep it going: each player has to recall all past items and add a new item. Continue until a player is unable to recall all items. Keep track as a group; count how many items were recalled before the game ended. Then play another round and try to do better each time. (It's OK to be silly with this game and take all kinds of wacky items!)

Assignment Idea #4:
Ready, Set, *GO for It!*

Executive Functions
- Working Memory
- Initiating Actions

RATIONALE: Not everyone is blessed with a good **working memory**. It is important to know the limits of one's ability to work from memory. With that understanding, we can either:

1) Use practice to improve our working memory, OR
2) Find ways to give our memories a boost or a reminder by using **cues** as *memory helpers.*

BENEFIT: This assignment helps the child test his or her working memory. It also helps the child to recognize the limits to his/her working memory and to use reminders, as needed, to get the job done.

MATERIALS NEEDED: Everyday objects

EXPLANATION FOR CHILD:

Sometimes we have to remember to do several things in a row. For example, when I go to the grocery store, I have to remember which things to get from the shelves. If there is just one thing to get, I don't need a grocery list, I just use my **memory**. *But if I have to get a lot of things, my memory needs a helper. So, I make a list. The list is a* **memory helper**.

Let's play a game called **Ready, Set, Go for It!** *Let's see how many things you can do from memory:*

> STEP 1: **READY =** *I'll tell you what to do.*
> STEP 2: **SET =** *You say back to me what you are supposed to do.*
> STEP 3: **GO FOR IT! =** *That's your cue to go ahead and* **do it.**

We'll start off easy and then get harder and harder. First, I'll give you just one thing to do. The next time I'll tell you two things. I will add one thing each time and we'll see how many things you can remember at once. When you get to where you have too many things to remember, we are going to use some **memory helpers***.*

Examples:

Trial A
Bring me the:
blue book by the phone.

Trial B
Bring me the:
red cup by the sink and the
newspaper from the coffee table.

Trial C
Bring me the:
book bag by the door
ruler from the desk, and the
apple from the bowl.

USING MEMORY HELPERS
When the child begins to have difficulty, teach the child to use **memory helpers.** Here's how: When you get to STEP 2 (**SET**) child decides on a memory helper to give external support to his/her working memory. Some possibilities are:

Memory Helper #1: Before you say **Go for It!**, have the child repeat the items aloud **three times** (instead of just once.)
Memory Helper #2: Before you say **Go for it!**, have the child make a list of the items. They can use words or draw quick pictures of the items. (You could also use the wrist checklist from the previous assignment.)
Memory Helper #3: Encourage the child to come up with his/her own memory helpers.

After deciding on a memory helper, go on to STEP 3 (**GO FOR IT!**). Then discuss: did the memory work? If not, try again, perhaps changing the memory helper to make if more effective.

ASSIGNMENT: The child and the coach can play this game at home. (See Tip and Variation on opposite page.)

Strategies for Success:
Setting Goals

The objective of the Simon Says program is to help children learn to improve their performance in everyday situations. To achieve this, the child and family make a plan to take the knowledge and skills they have learned in therapy sessions and apply them to everyday life.

Using the **Coach's Report** and the child's **Things to Do** list, goals can be put in writing. The more specific the goals, the easier it will be for the child to succeed in transferring these skills to day-to-day challenges. For example:

> **General goal:** *Mel will be ready for school on time.*
>
> **Specific goal #1:** *Mel will make 5 wrist checklists, one for every school day.*
>
> **Specific goal #2:** *Dad will give Mel a checklist 30 minutes before the bus arrives.*
>
> **Specific goal #3:** *Mel will complete the checklist in 15 minutes.*

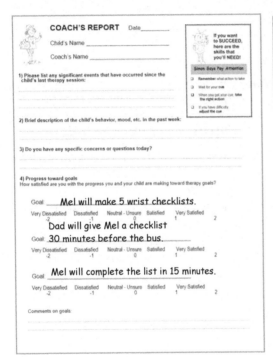 

COACHING TIP

Praise and encouragement can help children work hard toward goals. ***Behavior-specific praise*** is more effective than ***general praise*** because it reminds the child of the precise actions that led to success. Even if the child has experienced only partial success, highlighting what they did correctly can help build their confidence and motivate them to continue their effort.

General praise: *Good job, Mel.*

Behavior-specific praise: *Mel, the cue card you made looks really good! It's big and bright! You've almost solved the problem, you are so close! But you still forgot to turn off the light, so maybe putting it by the light switch wasn't the best spot for it. Can you think of a different place to put your card where you will be more likely to notice it?*

Behavior-specific praise: *Mel, you made that nice cue card, and decided to put it right there on the mirror and it worked! You figured out a way to help yourself remember to turn off the bathroom light. You're a good problem-solver.*

Strategies for Success:
Recognition and Encouragement

In this section, the child learns about **working memory** and about the strategy of using cues to support one's working memory. The therapist and coach should work closely together to encourage the child's intentions and efforts.

The **Yahoo!** materials in this section are one way to provide that recognition and encouragement in using strategies and tools to improve working memory.

The *Yahoo!* materials include these tools:

As soon as you got my signal that is was time to get ready for bed, you took the right action. Well done!

1. For the coach: **Encouraging Words**

This page gives examples of encouraging statements that the coach can make at the "point of performance" to acknowledge the child's progress and to direct attention, in positive ways, to areas that still need some improvement. (The therapist can also add other, more specific, statements to fit the needs of a particular child. See examples of behavior-specific praise in the Coaching Tip box on the preceding page.)

Copy the Encouraging Words page and give it to the coach as a reminder.

2. For other caretakers: **Skill Tracker**

The **Skill Tracker** form provides a way for adults other than the coach to recognize and encourage effort and progress. The form includes a copy of the *Skills Checklist* for working memory, plus a specific goal that the child is working on. For example, if Jack's grandmother takes care of him after school or on weekends, she might be involved in using the Secret-Signal Cue to remind Jack to flush the toilet. Jack's grandmother can complete a **Skill-Tracker** as a way to provide encouragement to Jack when he responds correctly to the secret cue.

3. For the therapist: *Good Job!* Tickets

The therapist can provide additional incentive to complete assignments by awarding the child *Good Job!* Tickets. The tickets include the checklist of working memory skills that the child is working on, giving the therapist an opportunity to provide behavior-specific praise.

If desired, the therapist can have the child periodically "cash in" the tickets for a reward provided by the therapist. (Have a variety of rewards: inexpensive prizes and/or special activities to do at the office.)

In the *Simon Says* program, the coach:

- Motivates the child by providing a vision of success.

- Creates interesting (and fun!) practice sessions.

- Sees that the child uses tools at the point of performance.

- **Recognizes even small signs of progress and provides encouragement.**

As your child tries out strategies to support their **working memory**, this page gives examples of encouraging statements that you can make to point out areas of progress. You can also direct attention, in positive ways, to areas that still need some improvement.

Add other statements to fit the needs of your child, making the statements as specific as possible. In other words, don't just say *"Good job!"* Tell the child exactly what they did right, even if it is just a small detail. Believe that your child wants to succeed and help them build on each small step.

If you want to SUCCEED, here are the skills that you'll NEED!

Simon Says Pay Attention

❑   **Remember** what action to take

❑   Wait for your **cue**

❑   When you get your cue, **take the right action**

❑   If you have difficulty, **adjust the cue**

Encouraging Words

Getting started

That will be a good cue to help your (or my) working memory. Let's start using it today.

You made a good plan to remind you what do do. Let's try it out and see how it works.

Troubleshooting

I know you want to do the right thing. Let's see if we can figure out a way to remind you when and where to take action.

That didn't work out today, but we can try again. Let's work on the cue and see if we can make it grab your attention."

Recognizing effort and success

You used your cues and finished (your homework/your chores). Now we have time to play a game.

As soon as you got my signal that is was time to (eat supper/get ready for bed) you took the right action. Well done!

Thanks for doing your part to get ready for (school/bed) on time. We are making some good changes in our home.

Skill Tracker

Thumbs up!
for

_____
(name)

If you want to SUCCEED, here are the skills that you'll NEED!

Simon Says Pay Attention

❑ **Remember** what action to take

❑ Wait for your **cue**

❑ When you get your cue, **take the right action**

❑ If you have difficulty, **adjust the cue**

Goal: _____

Date   What happened? (Tell how the skills were used.)

_____   _____

_____   _____

_____   _____

_____   _____

Good Job! Tickets

Copy and cut on dotted lines to make four tickets.

Use the tickets to reward and encourage the child's progress toward goals.

Put a checkmark by the skill (or skills) demonstrated and talk about the situation(s) in which it occurred.

This will help to raise the child's awareness of the specific behaviors that are helping them to succeed!

Summary
That's My Cue!

In this section, cues have been used primarily to remind the child to **initiate** actions that the child may be too distracted to remember to do. In the next chapter, we shift to **stopping** actions that interfere with overall intentions and goals

Before moving on to the next section (*Response Inhibition*) the child should be fairly skilled using cues as a reminder to do the right thing at the right time. The more comfortable and "expert" the child has become in using and strengthening cues, the easier it will be to apply these same concepts to a much more difficult challenge: stopping oneself from initiating one's automatic or impulsive response to a situation.

Simon Says Don't Do It!

Help Kids Improve Their

Response Inhibition

SECTION 2: *Don't Do It!*
(Response Inhibition)
Rationale for *Don't Do It!* Activities

What is the problem?

As noted in the previous section (*That's My Cue!*), children with ADHD may fail to get things done at the right time and in the right way. Cues can support the child's working memory, helping them remember what they are supposed to do, and prompting them to *initiate* the correct action.

However, to stay on-track and complete tasks on time, they must also *inhibit* other actions that distract them from their goal. For example, while initiating the actions involved in getting ready for school, the child must also inhibit their natural inclination to engage in other actions (watching TV, playing with a toy, reading a book) that would get them off-track and interfere with their intention to be ready on time.

Response inhibition is also very important in social situations, where one must often stop oneself from saying or doing whatever comes to mind. Most children with ADHD know how to act in social situations and fully intend to do so. But at the "point of performance," the child may react to a fleeting emotion or interest, get "off track," and fail to inhibit actions that are inappropriate for the situation.

What executive functions are involved?

The executive functions involved are those of:

- *Working memory* - keeping one's intentions in mind in order to reach one's goal

- *Inhibiting* - stopping responses that interfere with carrying out one's goal or intention

- *Internalized Speech* - "self-talk" to guide one's behavior

- *Self-monitoring* - checking on one's actions during an activity in order to stay on track

How can we provide external support for working memory?

1. Many traditional childhood games (Simon Says, Red Light - Green Light, Mother May I?) provide a fun way to practice response inhibition.

2. Children can learn:
   - To understand the difference between *on-track* and *off-track* behaviors.
   - To become more aware of when they are off-track.
   - To use self-talk to inhibit and re-direct their behavior.

Remember: To be effective, cues need to be at the point of performance.

Poor response inhibition (impulsivity) is one of the core difficulties for children with ADHD, causing the child to become distracted and off-task. To compensate for weak inhibition, they may need multiple forms of external support at the point of performance including:
- A visual reminder and/or plan (*Don't Do It* Cards and a *Stay-on-Track* Map)
- Use of "self talk" that reinforces response inhibition (telling oneself "Don't do it!")
- Cues from the coach that remind the child to STOP themselves from taking unwanted actions.

Overview of *Don't Do It!* Activities

	Activity or Assignment	Purpose	Page
STEP 1: **P**lay	***Simon Says Don't Do It!***	In this version of the traditional game ***Simon Says***, the child demonstrate his/her ability to inhibit behavior. The activity also introduces the concept of using "self-talk" to guide one's actions.	63
STEP 2: **L**ink	Story: ***The Distraction Zapper***	When Jacob goes to after-school care, he learns that he is not as good as his friends at staying "on task." When this causes him to lose out on having fun, Jacob learns to use **self-talk** to help him **inhibit behaviors** that get him off task.	67
	Worksheets	A review of the importance of being "on task" in everyday life.	70
STEP 3: **A**ssign	**The ON-OFF Switch**	Child practices inhibiting actions in response to tactile cues.	77
	Red Light, Green Light	Child practices inhibiting actions in response to verbal cues.	79
	***Don't Do It* cards**	The child makes a plan for inhibiting an unwanted behavior.	80
	The Stay-on-Track Map	For a particular situation, coach and child: 1. Make a visual "map" of on-track and off-track behaviors 2. Agree on a cue that the coach will use if the child gets off track (Note: This assignment introduces the concept of self-monitoring, which will be expanded in the next section. The map provides an **external plan** for behavior. The coach helps the child monitor his or her adherence to the plan.)	85
STEP 4: **Y**ahoo!	Encouraging Words Skill Tracker *Good Job!*	Adults provide feedback and encouragement as the child tries out new strategies and tools to improve response inhibition.	89

If you want to SUCCEED, here are the skills that you'll NEED!

Simon Says *Don't Do It!*

- ❑ **Do** what you are supposed to do. (Stay **on task.**)
- ❑ **Don't do** anything that you are not supposed to do. (Don't be **off task.**)
- ❑ If you start to get distracted, tell Yourself, "**Don't Do It!**"
- ❑ If you notice you are off task, **STOP** right away.

Play Intervention:
Simon Says *Don't Do It!*

In the game outlined on the next three pages (a version of the traditional childhood game *Simon Says*) the child demonstrates his/her ability to **inhibit behavior.** The activity also introduces the concept of using "self-talk" to guide one's actions.

Begin by giving the child a copy of the checklist on this page. The checklist explains what the child needs to do to succeed at playing *Simon Says Don't Do It*. Go over the checklist with the child *before* playing the game and use it again to review *after* playing the game.

The purpose of the game is to show the child that he/she can already perform these skills in the context of play. In the steps following this **P**lay activity (**L**ink, **A**ssign, and **Y**ahoo!) the child and coach will learn strategies and tools that will help the child perform these skills in other contexts in day-to-day life.

If you want to SUCCEED, here are the skills that you'll NEED!

Simon Says *Don't Do It!*

- ❑ **Do** what you are supposed to do. (Stay **on task.**)
- ❑ **Don't do** anything that you are not supposed to do. (Don't be **off task.**)
- ❑ If you start to get distracted, tell Yourself, "**Don't Do It!**"
- ❑ If you notice you are off task, **STOP** right away.

If you want to SUCCEED, here are the skills that you'll NEED!

Simon Says *Don't Do It!*

- ❑ **Do** what you are supposed to do. (Stay **on task.**)
- ❑ **Don't do** anything that you are not supposed to do. (Don't be **off task.**)
- ❑ If you start to get distracted, tell Yourself, "**Don't Do It!**"
- ❑ If you notice you are off task, **STOP** right away.

Simon Says *Don't Do It!* (Part 1)

Materials: None needed. (Part 1 is just an introduction; don't use the skill checklist until Part 2)

Get Ready: Tell the child:

> The name of this activity is **Simon Says Don't Do It!** In this game, what you **Don't Do** is very, very important. You have to be very careful that you **Don't Do** the wrong thing—because guess what happens if you do?(…You have to go back and start all over again!)

Get Set: "Simon" stands on one side of the room (Finish Line) and the child stands on the other end of the room (Starting Line).

Go: "Simon" gives a series of commands such as: *Take three baby steps forward, Jump up and down, Twirl around, Take one giant step forward, Pat your head, Rub your tummy, Take two bunny hops forward,* etc.

Sometimes, Simon should begin the command with the magic words, ***Simon Says.*** Sometimes, Simon will just give the command without saying the magic words.

The child is to follow the command only when it is preceded by the magic words, ***Simons Says***.

If the child follows the command without the magic words, they have to go back to the start line and begin again.

Note: Go slowly and give the child a chance to succeed. However, try to "trick" the child into taking at least one wrong move, so that they have the experience of going back to the Start Line. Try to do this early on and then follow up more slowly, giving the child a chance to succeed. If the child starts to do the "wrong thing" and then stops, comment on this:

> *Good job! You remembered and you stopped yourself from doing that. You are really paying close attention!*

Review: Tell the child:

> *You did a great job. You understand that sometimes what you don't do is very, very important. Sometimes you almost did the wrong thing, but then you remembered and you stopped yourself.*
>
> (Give specific example.)
>
> *That was excellent. Are you ready to make the game a little harder?*

Simon Says *Don't Do It!* (Part 2)

Materials: Skill checklist on page 62.

> If you want to SUCCEED, here are the skills that you'll NEED!
>
> **Simon Says *Don't Do It!***
>
> ☐ ***Do*** what you are supposed to do. (Stay **on task**.)
> ☐ ***Don't do*** anything that you are not supposed to do. (Don't be **off task**.)
> ☐ If you start to get distracted, tell Yourself, "***Don't Do It!***"
> ☐ If you notice you are off task, **STOP** right away.

Get Ready: Tell the child:

> *We are going to play* **Simon Says** *again and we are going to do a few things differently. You'll need some special skills to win at this game. Let's look at the skills checklist.*

Get Set: Read over the checklist and give a copy to the child.

> *In this game, I am going to try really, really, really hard to trick you. Whenever I tell you to do something without saying, "**Simon Says**," I want you to whisper to yourself, "**Don't do it!**"*

Go: Have the child practice doing this. The whisper needs to be loud enough for you to hear.

> *In this game, if you move at the wrong time* **OR** *if you forget to whisper "Don't Do It!" you will have to go back to the starting line.*

"Simon" stands on one side of the room (Finish Line) and the child stands on the other end of the room (Starting Line).

In this version, Simon tries harder to trick the child. Some ways to do this are:
1) Sometimes begin the command with similar but different words.
   (*Slimon Says, Pimon Says, Simon Suggests, Simon wants you to...*)
2) Sometimes begin with the child's name. (*Marie, take one giant step forward.*)

Remember: The purpose of this game is to have the child use "self-talk" as an aid to inhibiting behavior. Respond to their actions in ways that raise their awareness of this strategy.

1) If the child remembers to whisper "*Don't Do It*," be sure to acknowledge this:
> *Good job, you told yourself just what to do...*

2) If the child starts to do the "wrong thing" and then stops and whispers "*Don't Do It*," comment on this:
> *Good job! You told yourself to* **stop** *just in time.*

3) If the child fails to inhibit their behavior, or fails to whisper "*Don't Do It*," comment on this:
> *Uh-oh, what did you forget to do? It's back to the starting line!*
> *Let's practice together. What do we need to tell ourselves when there is something we are not supposed to do?*
> > (Practice together. Feel free to ham it up and be silly; make the game fun, even if the child has to start over again. For example, the two of you might practice saying "***Don't Do It!***" in three different kinds of voices.)

 Play

COACHING TIP

It's Child's Play!

Traditional childhood games such as **Simon Says** and **Red-Light Green-Light** are often thought of as simply pleasant ways for children to pass the time. But in actuality, these games that children love to play are supporting the development of important executive functions. Children are drawn to activities that foster their development and it's no coincidence that these activities become popular with children at the same time that "real life" is demanding greater skills from them. *Working memory* and *response inhibition* are critical to success in playing these games and are also critical for following a teacher's instructions at school. The social and fun nature of these childhood games motivate children to practice these skills over and over! So, have fun and play with your child. Not only do these fun times build positive bonds, they help children gain better attention and self-control skills!

COACHING TIP

Make this story come alive!

The story on the next page is written so that it can be read aloud as a "play."

There are five parts in this story. They are:
1) **Narrator**
2) **Jacob**
3) **Paul**
4) **Joni**
5) **Al**

To make the parts easier to read, make a copy of the story for each reader. On each copy, highlight the part(s) to be performed by that reader.

Have fun!

If you want to SUCCEED, here are the skills that you'll NEED!

Simon Says *Don't Do It!*

- ☐ ***Do*** what you are supposed to do. (Stay **on task**.)
- ☐ ***Don't do*** anything that you are not supposed to do. (Don't be **off task**.)
- ☐ If you start to get distracted, tell yourself, ***"Don't Do It!"***
- ☐ If you notice you are off task, STOP right away.

When do people use these skills in Real Life?

When Jacob goes to after-school care, he learns that he is not as good as his friends at staying "on-task."

When this causes him to lose out on having fun, Jacob learns to use *self-talk* to help him inhibit behaviors that get him off-task.

The Distraction Zapper

MONDAY

Narrator: Jacob's mom started a new job, so Monday was his first day to attend the After-School Camp. His friends, Paul and Joni, had told him about playing ball at the camp. Jacob couldn't wait! When he got to the gym, Jacob was surprised when his friends sat down and pulled out homework.

Jacob: Hey, I thought we were going to play ball!

Paul: Yeah, we are, but we have to do homework first. That's the rule.

Narrator: Paul got to work right away. Jacob slowly pulled out his books. He hated doing homework! At home, his dad always helped him. Jacob took out his math homework. He didn't have a pencil.

Joni: There are extra school supplies on that table over there.

Narrator: Jacob walked across the gym. He stopped to watch two counselors getting bats and balls out of a closet. He went to the supply table and chose a pencil. Then he went to the water fountain and got a drink. When he got back to his table, Paul had already finished his homework and was heading outside with one of the counselors, carrying a bat. Jacob looked at Joni.

Jacob: Man, how did Paul finish so fast?

Joni: Oh, he's a master at staying on task. Not me; I get off task a lot. I think I'll go sit on the bleachers so I can concentrate better.

Narrator: Jacob worked on his first math problem. Then he remembered that he had a new pen. He opened up his backpack. He saw his baseball cards. He got them out and began to arrange them. A little later, Joni tossed her spelling notebook on the table.

Joni: Hey, that was easier than I thought. Are you ready to go outside?

Narrator: Jacob looked down at his *one* completed math problem. He told Joni to he'd be out soon.

TUESDAY

Paul: Hey, why didn't you come outside yesterday?

Jacob: I didn't finish my stupid homework.

Paul: Well, get it done today. We need you on our team!

Narrator: Jacob told Paul he'd get it done. He decided to do what Joni had done, and took his math homework to the bleachers. Jacob had two problems done when he glanced under the bleachers. He saw some coins! He climbed down, and picked up the money. Then he went and talked with Al, the counselor.

Jacob: Can I keep this money I found?

Al: Sure! Finders, keepers.

Jacob: Can I use it in the snack machine?

Al: I guess so. But didn't you just have a snack?

PAGE 2

Jacob: Yeah, but I like using the snack machine.

Al: Well, if that's what you want to do. It's your choice, man.

Narrator: Jacob ran to the snack machine. It was hard to decide! He finally chose some cheese crackers. He went back to his table and looked for his spelling work. It was gone--someone must have taken it! Then he remembered. He had taken it to the bleachers. Yes, there it was. Jacob got to work. But before he finished, the ball players came back inside. Ball time was over.

WEDNESDAY

Jacob: I hate this camp!

Narrator: That's what Jacob thought on Wednesday when, for the third day, he watched his friends leave to play ball. He put his head down on the table. Then he heard someone speak. It was Al, the counselor.

Al: Hi Jacob. Can we talk?

Jacob: Sure, why not? I might as well talk, 'cause I'm never going to get to play ball.

Al: You're a lot like me. You have a hard time staying on-task because you get distracted easily, don't you?

Jacob: Yeah, I guess so.

Al: What you need is ...a *Distraction Zapper*.

Narrator: Al held out his hand as if he was holding a remote control.

Al: When I am trying to get something done, and I get off task, I pull out my handy Distraction Zapper. Let's say I'm cleaning my room, and then I start to think about eating potato chips.

Narrator: Al pointed his hand to a bag of chips on the table and whispered...

Al: *Zap!*...You see, when I say "*Zap,*" those chips lose their power to distract me. And I'm back on-task.

Jacob: You don't really think an imaginary zapper will help me get my homework done, do you?

Al: You never know until you try. You may be surprised, Jacob.

Narrator: Jacob sighed. "*Al is crazy,*" he decided. Back at the bleachers, he finished one math problem. He glanced under the bleachers and saw a baseball cap. He climbed down and was about to reach for the cap when he caught Al's eye. Al lifted his hand and pointed his "zapper" at Jacob and smiled. Jacob laughed and looked again at the baseball cap. Then he pointed toward the cap and whispered:

Jacob: *Zap! Quit distracting me.*

Narrator: Jacob felt kind of silly, talking to a cap, but it worked! He left the cap there and finished his math. He looked at the clock. He was doing great. He put his math book in his back pack. His baseball cards were still there. He took one out and started reading it. Just then Al walked by. Al looked at the cards and then at Jacob. He held out his hand.

Al: Do you need to borrow my zapper?

Jacob: That's OK, Al. I've got my own. I'm getting back on task right now.

Narrator: Jacob pointed to the baseball card. *Zap!* Then he finished his spelling, put his books away and headed outside. Paul and Joni saw Jacob come out to the field.

Paul: Come on, Jacob! We've been waiting for you. We need you on our team!

Narrator: Jacob ran to join them, smiling. He thought to himself:

Jacob: *I guess Al isn't so crazy after all. Maybe tomorrow I can be the first one out instead of the last. I'll just have to keep my Distraction Zapper handy!*

The Distraction Zapper
Questions for Discussion

Joni said that Paul was a master at staying "on task." What did she mean?

Was Jacob being slow on purpose? (Explain your answer.)

At first, Jacob thought that Al's idea was weird. Why did he decide to try it?

Extra Questions

Two times, Al gave Jacob a **cue** to remind him that he was off-task. What were the cues?

Pretend that you are writing "Chapter 2" of Jacob's . story. What would happen in Chapter 2?

Tell about a time that you were distracted and got off-task.

If you want to SUCCEED, here are the skills that you'll NEED!

Simon Says Don't Do It!

❑ **Do** what you are supposed to do. (Stay **on task**.)

❑ **Don't do** anything that you are not supposed to do. (Don't be **off task**.)

❑ If you start to get distracted, tell Yourself, "**Don't Do It!**"

❑ If you notice you are off task, **STOP** right away.

Internalized Speech means using "self-talk" to guide your actions.

• In the game *Simon Says Don't Do It!*, players use the words, "*Don't Do It*," as a guide to inhibiting the undesired actions.

• In the story *The Distraction Zapper*, Jacob uses the word, "*Zap*," along with other words *("Quit distracting me")* to guide himself and inhibit the behavior that was interfering with his goal.

• In the assignment, *Red Light–Green Light* (Page 79), the term "*Red Light*" is used as a cue to inhibit behavior.

    Each child can be encouraged to come up with the one or more terms that he or she can use as **self-talk** to help inhibit undesired behaviors.

If you want to SUCCEED, here are the skills that you'll NEED!

Simon Says *Don't Do It!*

- ❏ **Do** what you are supposed to do. (Stay **on task**.)
- ❏ **Don't do** anything that you are not supposed to do. (Don't be **off task**.)
- ❏ If you start to get distracted, tell Yourself, "**Don't Do It!**"
- ❏ If you notice you are off task, **STOP** right away.

When do people use these skills in Real Life?

Person	Do It! On-task behaviors	Don't Do It! Off-task behaviors	What happens if they get off-task?
Person driving a car down a busy street			
Baseball player in the outfield waiting to catch a ball			
Grandmother making the birthday cake for her grandchild's party that afternoon			
Santa loading his sleigh on Christmas Eve			
School bus driver on his way to pick up children to go on a field trip			

If you want to SUCCEED, here are the skills that you'll NEED!

Simon Says *Don't Do It!*

☐ **Do** what you are supposed to do. (Stay **on task.**)

☐ **Don't do** anything that you are not supposed to do. (Don't be **off task.**)

☐ If you start to get distracted, tell Yourself, *"Don't Do It!"*

☐ If you notice you are off task, **STOP** right away.

Link

When do people use these skills in Real Life?

How about <u>YOU</u>?

When do you need to use these skills in Real Life?

What is an activity or job that you do *very* well? (Examples: play soccer, take care of baby brother, fold clothes, make friends.)

_____

When you are on-task for that activity or job, what do you do?

1) _____

2) _____

3) _____

What are some behaviors that would be off-task for that activity or job?

1) _____

2) _____

3) _____

What would happen if you stayed off-task for that activity or job?

_____

Point of Performance and the Coach's Role

Because of the importance of using interventions at the **point of performance**, the role of the "coach" is an integral part of the *Simon Says Pay Attention* program. At home, a parent or other adult can act as coach. In a school setting, a teacher or other staff member can act as coach at the point of performance.

Using the Coach's Report

It is important to have good communication between the therapist and the coach, so that the therapist can make adjustments to the program based on the particular needs of the child and the family (and/or classroom). The Coach's Report on the next page provides a concise way to keep the therapist and coach "on the same page" as the child progresses through the Simon Says program.

- We recommend that the therapist introduce the use of the **Coach's Report** during the **Link** activities and continue to use the reports as part of the **Assign** activities.

- The therapist can help the child and coach formulate goals during the therapy session, writing them directly on the **Coach's Report.**

- The **Coach's Report** can then go home with the coach at the end of each session.

- At the next session, the coach returns the completed form to the therapist prior to the start of the session.

- In addition to showing the progress the child has made on the goals, the report will update the therapist on any significant events that have occurred since the last session and any special concerns that need to be addressed.

The **Coach's Report** on the opposite page is specific for Part 2 of the Simon Says program. Use the *Don't Do It!* checklist to help formulate goals that are related to **response inhibition.**

Improving response inhibition is not easy, so start with some basic goals. Initially, suggest that the coach and child use play to give the child an opportunity to practice response inhibition. Also consider goals to help the child become more aware of when and where it is important to "stop yourself" in real life. For example:

Goal: _Play Simon Says Don't Do It at home._

Goal: _Tell about a time someone STOPPED doing something in order to stay on task._

COACH'S REPORT   Date_____

Child's Name _____

Coach's Name _____

> **If you want to SUCCEED, here are the skills that you'll NEED!**
>
> **Simon Says Don't Do It!**
>
> ❑ **Do** what you are supposed to do. (Stay **on task**.)
> ❑ **Don't do** anything that you are not supposed to do. (Don't be **off task**.)
> ❑ If you start to get distracted, tell Yourself, "**Don't Do It!**"
> ❑ If you notice you are off task, **STOP** right away.

1) Please list any significant events that have occurred since your child's last therapy session:

....

....

....

....

2) Brief description of your child's behavior, mood, etc. in the past week:

....

....

....

3) Do you have any specific concerns or questions today?

....

....

....

4) Progress toward goals

Goal: _____

Very Dissatisfied	Dissatisfied	Neutral - Unsure	Satisfied	Very Satisfied
-2	-1	0	1	2

Goal: _____

Very Dissatisfied	Dissatisfied	Neutral - Unsure	Satisfied	Very Satisfied
-2	-1	0	1	2

Goal: _____

Very Dissatisfied	Dissatisfied	Neutral - Unsure	Satisfied	Very Satisfied
-2	-1	0	1	2

Comments on goals:

....

....

....

Things to Do:

Name: _____

Date: _____

If you want to SUCCEED, here are the skills that you'll NEED!

Simon Says *Don't Do It!*

- ❏ **Do** what you are supposed to do. (Stay **on task**.)
- ❏ **Don't do** anything that you are not supposed to do. (Don't be **off task**.)
- ❏ If you start to get distracted, tell Yourself, *"Don't Do It!"*
- ❏ If you notice you are off task, **STOP** right away.

_____

_____

_____

_____

_____

GOOD JOB

REMEMBER:

You've got the skills

that you need to succeed!

| Assignment Idea # 1 | ## The ON-OFF Switch |

This activity is a variation of the childhood game of *Statues*. Although this seems like an extremely simple activity, what is being practiced here–**inhibiting Behavior**–is an ability that is essential in many situations. As the child demonstrates this ability within the structure of a game, they become aware that they can make a conscious choice to control their actions.

A secondary benefit is that, since the child responds to a **tactile cue** (a touch on the shoulder) to inhibit behavior, this same cue can be used by a parent or teacher in other situations in which the child needs to inhibit actions.

Page 77

| Assignment Idea # 2 | ## Red Light, Green Light |

In Assignment #1, the child practices inhibiting behavior in response to a tactile cue. In this assignment, the child responds to a **verbal cue** (the words *Red Light*). This can be played as the traditional childhood game of Red Light, Green Light, or adapted for a variety of other activities. As with all assignments, providing variety keeps the activities fresh and makes them more fun.

The same cue used in this activity, the term *Red Light*, can also be used by the parent in other situations as a reminder to the child to stop a certain behavior.

Page 79

| Assignment Idea # 3 | ## *Don't Do It!* Cards |

With the *Don't Do It! Cards*, the child and coach connect the concept of response inhibition to everyday life and set personal intentions to stop selected behaviors.

Page 81

| Assignment Idea # 4 | ## The Stay-On-Track Map |

In this assignment the child and coach create a visual plan to identify on-track and off-track behaviors in a particular situation. They also agree on a **cue** that can be used to remind the child to get back "on track."

Page 85

 Use the **Things to Do** list to give the child a written reminder of the assignment.

COACHING TIP

Helpful Hint for the *ON-OFF Switch* Assignment:
In doing this assignment at home, keep this activity FUN! Stop long before the child becomes tired of it. Practice this frequently, but for short periods of time.

Praise the child, using language that focuses on the skill of stopping the action immediately in response to the cue.
- *You stopped right on cue–that was perfect timing.*
- *You are remembering to think, "Don't Do It!"*

Assignment Idea #1:
The ON-OFF Switch

Executive Functions
- Response inhibition
- Internalized speech
- Self-monitoring

RATIONALE: To be successful in many activities, children need to be able to *inhibit* behaviors that are not pertinent to the given activity.

BENEFIT: This activity is a variation of the childhood game of *Statues*. Although this seems like an extremely simple activity, what is being practiced here--**inhibiting behavior**--is an ability that is essential in many situations. As the child demonstrates this ability within the structure of a game, they become aware that they can make a conscious choice to control their actions.

A secondary benefit is that, since the child responds to a **tactile cue** (a touch on the shoulder), this same cue can be used by a parent or teacher in other situations in which the child needs to inhibit actions. (Assignment Idea #2, Red Light-Green Light, is very similar but uses words rather than touch as the cue. It can be helpful to have the child learn to respond to both verbal and tactile cues.)

MATERIALS NEEDED: None.

EXPLANATION FOR CHILD:

> *Remember that sometimes what you **don't do** is just as important as what you **do**. In this assignment, you practice switching between **Do** and **Don't Do** whenever you get a special cue. In this game, the cue isn't one that you hear or see; it is one that you feel.*

ASSIGNMENT:

> *Your assignment is to do an activity called The ON-OFF Switch. We will play the game now and then you can play it again later with your coach to get more practice.*
>
> *In this game, one person is the Museum Director. Everyone else is a statue at the museum. These are very special statues. They can move, but only when the Director turns them ON by pressing the "switch" on their shoulders. And as soon as the Director turns them OFF, they immediately turn back into regular statues.*

> **Ask permission to touch child on shoulder and then demonstrate:**
> **the first touch means _ON/Go_, the second touch means _OFF/Stop_.**

> *Each player gets to decide what kind of statue to be (Dancer, Baseball Player, Cook, Parent with Baby, Musician, Teacher, Traffic Cop, etc.) The Museum Director visits each statue, turns it ON, and watches the statue move. The Museum Director guesses what kind of statue that person is. The Director gets to decide when to turn the statue OFF, and presses the ON-OFF switch again. Each statue has to stop immediately and hold perfectly still when it is in OFF mode.*

> **Demonstrate for the child, using an example such as Cook: the Cook might chop vegetables, add water to a pot, stir, smell the aroma, taste with a spoon, add some spices, etc. When the Cook statue receives the OFF cue, it must stop in mid-action.**

COACH'S ROLE: The coach should set up practice sessions at home. (See suggestions on preceding page.)

COACHING TIP

Helpful Hint for the *Red Light/Green Light* Assignment:
As with the preceding assignment, keep this activity FUN by playing for **short** periods.

Parents might also try using this same technique with simple chores (such as setting the table, feeding the dog, folding clothes.) Here's how:

- Make the *Green Light* times longer.
- When the coach says *Red Light*, the child must pause all action.
- Use the pause to recognize what the child has done thus far in completing the chore. Show your appreciation!
- Give a big *Yahoo!* when the chore is done.

Assign

Assignment Idea #2:
Red Light/Green Light

Executive Functions
- Response inhibition
- Internalized speech
- Self-monitoring

RATIONALE: To be successful in many activities, children need to be able to *inhibit* behaviors that are not pertinent to the given activity.

BENEFIT: This is a traditional childhood game. Although this seems like an extremely simple activity, what is being practiced here–**inhibiting behavior**–is an ability that is essential in many situations. As the child demonstrates this ability within the structure of a game, he/she becomes aware that it is possible to make a conscious choice to control one's actions.

A secondary benefit is that, since the child responds to a **verbal cue** (the words *Red Light*), this same cue can be used by a parent or teacher in other situations in which the child needs to inhibit actions. (Assignment Idea #1, The ON-OFF Switch, is very similar but uses touch rather than words as the cue. It can be helpful to have the child learn to respond to both verbal and tactile cues.)

MATERIALS NEEDED: No materials. A large room or long hallway is needed to have sufficient room for the standard play. However, see *VARIATIONS* (below) for ways to play in a smaller space.

EXPLANATION FOR CHILD:

*Remember that sometimes what you **don't do** is just as important as what you **do**. In this game, you have to switch from **Do** to **Don't Do** whenever you hear a special cue. The cue to switch from **Do** to **Don't Do** is the words **"Red Light."***

ASSIGNMENT:

*Your assignment is to do an activity called **Red Light/Green Light**. We will practice the game right now and then you can play with your coach later. In this game, one person is the Stop Light and stands at one end of the room (or hall). The other players stand at the opposite end. When the Stop Light says, "**Green Light**," the players can walk, hop on one foot, jump, skip, or crawl toward the Stop Light. At any time, the Stop Light can say, "**Red Light**." Then the players have to STOP exactly where they are, even if in mid-movement.*

(Demonstrate.)

*If they move at all after, "**Red Light**," is called, they have to start over. Then the Stop Light says "**Green Light**," and the players can move again until the next time,"**Red Light**," is called. The first player to get to the Stop Light is the winner. That player becomes the Stop Light.*

VARIATIONS

1) The players engage in some sort of activity: it could be eating a snack, building with blocks, or putting together a puzzle. They begin when the Stop Light says, "Green Light,"and must stop immediately when they hear the cue, "Red Light." Since there is no clear end point in this game, just play for a while, and when the child shows mastery, switch roles.

2) Make the game more challenging (and silly) by substituting similar sounding words for *Green Light* and *Red Light*. (*Green Grass, Green Tight, Red Bed, Red Fight*.)

COACH'S ROLE: The coach should set up practice sessions at home.
(See suggestions on preceding page.)

It's fun to play games like **Simon Says** and **Red-Light Green-Light.** While game play helps children **understand** the concept of response inhibition, it will not necessarily improve their response inhibition in day to day life. It's very difficult to apply this concept to everyday life because we so often respond to a given situation with an ingrained, automatic response. Breaking through this habit requires 1st, setting an intention to change, and 2nd, motivating oneself to follow through on that intention.

COACHING TIP

Intention and Motivation

***Don't Do It!* Ca**rds are a way of expressing an intention to stop doing something and putting that intention in writing. The cards can then be posted as reminders of our intentions, motivating us to follow through.

We highly recommend that both the coach and the child carry out this assignment. Children benefit from knowing that habit change is something that is difficult for adults as well as children. It takes **determination** and **persistence**, so set an intention for yourself and model those qualities for your child!

Assign

Assignment Idea #3:
Don't Do It! Cards

Executive Functions
- Response inhibition
- Internalized speech
- Self-monitoring

RATIONALE: It can be difficult to apply the principle of response inhibition in everyday life because we may habitually respond to a given situation with an automatic response that is not helpful. Most children can readily understand the *need* to inhibit certain behaviors in everyday life. However, being able to actually inhibit those habitual responses can be very difficult (even for adults). Everyone can benefit from interventions designed to foster motivation and bolster good intentions.

BENEFIT: With this activity, children:
- discuss the importance of ***inhibiting actions*** that are not appropriate or helpful to a given situation.
- receive encouragement and support from therapist and parent(s).
- reflect on the importance of this ability in their everyday lives and identify situations in which they might benefit from response inhibition.
- make a commitment to trying to modify at least one unwanted behavior.

MATERIALS NEEDED: *Don't Do It!* Cards (Page 83)

1. EXPLANATION FOR CHILD:

After playing *Simon Says Don't Do It!, The ON-OFF Switch,* and *Red Light/ Green Light,* the therapist can help the child recognize the benefits of telling ourselves "Don't Do It!" in everyday life. Review the Skills Checklist (page 62).

With all of these games, the way to win is by stopping yourself from doing something at the wrong time. It's not easy; you have to really pay attention and really want to stop yourself. Sometimes, in real life, we have to stop ourselves, too. That can be harder than in a game.

The therapist can tell the child that adults as well as children benefit from stopping themselves and offer some examples from his or her everyday life (keeping them simple and generic.) For example:

Yesterday I went to the cabinet and got a bag of cookies. I opened the bag up. Then I stopped. I remembered that I had promised myself not to eat sweets between meals. Even though I had already opened the bag, I stopped in the middle (just like we did when we played Red-Light, Green Light). Then I closed up the bag and put it back in the cabinet. It was hard, but I felt happy because I know that I will be healthier and feel better if I stop myself form eating sweets between meals.

Note: The preceding example focuses on stopping ***one's actions,*** as in the games. The next example focuses on stopping ***one's thoughts.***

*I was driving and someone pulled right in front of me. I had to slam on my brakes. I started to think what a jerk that person was and that people like that shouldn't be allowed to drive! But then I told myself, "**Don't Do It!**," just like we did when we played Simon Says. Instead, I thought to myself, "I'm glad I saw him in time to step on the brake." If I'd kept thinking about that driver, I would have felt angry and upset. Maybe I would have cursed and pounded on the steering wheel. But I stopped those thoughts and focused on different thoughts. And then I did something that helped me feel much better: I took a deep breath, and I turned on some music.*

The child's parents can be asked to offer examples of times in their lives when they need to stop themselves from doing and/or thinking something. Encourage them to also discuss the benefits. Finally, have the child offer some examples of times that he or she could benefit from stopping themselves from doing and/or thinking something. Emphasize the benefits: short and long term, and benefits for others as well as for oneself.

                    Continued on next page.

Don't Do It! Cards (Continued)

2. SET INTENTIONS:

An essential step in CBT is planning how to apply the strategies learned in therapy to everyday life. This plan can start with the simple act of having the child make *Don't Do It!* Cards to set their intentions. Explain to the family:

It was fun stopping ourselves when we played the games, but in real life, it can be hard to stop doing certain things. It's always good to have a reminder, so I want you to think of some things that you want to remember not to do and write them down on these cards.

Provide them with cards and have them each set at least one intention and write it on a card. If they want to do more than one intention, each should be on a separate card.

3. PLAN WAYS TO SUPPORT THOSE INTENTIONS:

Children are likely to need a lot of external support to carry out their intentions. Therefore, the child's plan should also include some means of providing that support. One way is to set up "cues" as reminders. Review with the child what a cue is and say:

*The best place to get a cue is at the very moment that we want to stop ourselves from doing something. I made a **Don't Do It!** Card that said, "No sweets between meals," and I put it on the cabinet where the cookies are. So, when I'm feeling hungry and go to the cabinet to get a cookie, the card is a cue right there to remind me to stop. What about you; can you think of a good place to put your card so that it can be a reminder?*

Help the family to brainstorm for ideas of where to place the card so it can be a cue. If the situation doesn't lend itself having a visual reminder, suggest that the card be put somewhere where the child will see it in the morning. Then talk about other types of "cues" that family members can give to one another.

The cards are one type of cue to help us remember our intentions. One nice thing about being part of a family is that we can help one another remember what it is we are trying to do. Is there a way that someone in your family can give you a signal that can be a cue for you to stop yourself?

Have the family brainstorm ideas. For example, perhaps the words, *"Red Light,"* could be a verbal cue. Or, they may prefer some other sort of "secret signal." Whatever the plan, emphasize that this is the child's plan:

    1) the child has set an intention to refrain from some habitual response;

    2) the child has outlined the benefits to come from following through on this intention; and

    3) the child has planned for (and perhaps asked for) support in carrying out this plan.

Note: As with any home assignment, it is important that the therapist follow up at the next session, celebrate if the child has been successful, and provide troubleshooting and encouragement if the child had difficulty following through.

Creating a *stay-on-track map*

    1) helps the child to state their intention in specific terms and

    2) provides a visual reminder of those intentions.

As with all assignments, implementation at the ***point of performance*** can be challenging. If your child has made a map, but is not able to follow through in the real-life circumstances, stay positive! Compliment your child on the thought and effort that went into creating the map. Let your child know that setting the right intentions is the first step and that you and the therapist will help the child figure out a way to successfully carry out those intentions.

Planning for Success

COACHING TIP On the back of the map, jot down details to discuss with your child's therapist. Do this with the child's input (after things have calmed down). Avoid scolding. Instead, focus on

    1) the good intentions that your child set,

    2) what actually happened (start with the positive) and

    3) your child's ideas about what might help next time.

After your child has listed their ideas, offer an idea or two of your own. Tell your child that the two of you will bring the list of ideas to the next therapy session and see what ideas the therapist has. Then, with all of those ideas, the child can decide which ideas will help the most.

Through this process, you will be teaching your child crucial life lessons about problem-solving and persistence!

Assignment Idea # 4:
The Stay-on-Track Map

Executive Functions
- Response inhibition
- Internalized speech
- Self-monitoring

RATIONALE: To be successful in many activities, children need to be able to *inhibit* behaviors that are either not pertinent or not appropriate. The concepts of **on-task** and **off-task** (or **on-track** and **off-track**) can give the child a helpful framework for thinking about what behaviors are desirable in a given situation. The child's own heightened awareness, along with cues from others, can help the child inhibit behaviors that lead them off-track.

BENEFIT: In this assignment the child and coach create an **external plan** (a map) to identify on-track and off-track behaviors in a particular situation. They also agree on a **cue** to be used to remind the child to get back "on track."
Examples of situations in which a map might be used are:

1. The child has difficulty completing tasks on time because he/she gets distracted and does other things that are not pertinent to the task.

2. The child has difficulty in social situations (visiting relatives, going to the store) because he/she does things that are inappropriate for the situation or are annoying to others.

MATERIALS NEEDED: The Stay-on-Track Map on the next page.

EXPLANATION FOR CHILD:

*Remember the story about Jacob and **The Distraction Zapper**? In that story, Jacob's goal is to finish his homework and play ball with his friends. He learns that what he* **doesn't do** *is just as important as what he* **does**. *So, when he notices himself doing something he shouldn't, he tells himself to STOP. After he stops, he can get back* **on track** *toward his goal.*

- *When Jacob gets off track, his counselor, Al, gives him something. What is it?*
  (Al gives Jacob a **cue** to remind him to STOP what he is doing and get back on-track.)
- *What are the things that Jacob has* **to do** *to stay on track?*
  (Do his math, do his spelling, etc.)
- *What are the things that Jacob has to* **not do**—*things that get him* **off track?**
  (Playing with his baseball cards, climbing under the bleachers, etc.)

ASSIGNMENT:

In this assignment, you are going to make a map to help you stay on track.

If Jacob made a **Stay-on-Track Map**, *it might look this:*

(Assignment continued on the next page.)

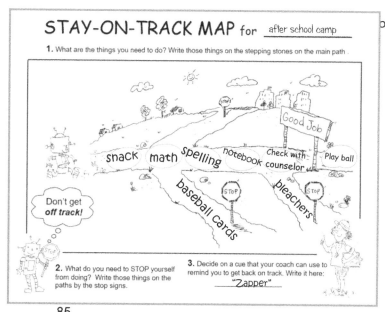

STAY-ON-TRACK MAP for _after school camp_

1. What are the things you need to do? Write those things on the stepping stones on the main path.

Good Job

snack   math   Spelling   notebook   Check with counselor   Play ball

STOP

baseball cards   STOP   bleachers   STOP

Don't get **off track!**

2. What do you need to STOP yourself from doing? Write those things on the paths by the stop signs.

3. Decide on a cue that your coach can use to remind you to get back on track. Write it here:
"Zapper"

The Stay-on-Track Map (Continued)

ASSIGNMENT: In this assignment, the child and coach make a **Stay-on-Track Map** to help the child stay "on track" for a particular situation. (See examples below and on previous page, then use map on page 87.)

Here's how:
1. Copy and cut out a blank **Stay-on-Track Map** (page 87).
2. On the stepping stones, help the child write the actions they need to take to stay **on track** in that situation.
3. On the paths by the STOP signs, write some actions that would be **off track** for that situation. Encourage the child to remember that, if they get off-track, they can STOP and tell themselves, "**Don't Do It!**"
4. Decide on a **cue** that the coach can use if the child gets off track. Write the cue in the lower-right corner.

Example of a Stay-on-Track Map for **getting ready for school in the morning.**

The goal in this plan is to be ready on time, or perhaps even a bit early, so the child has time to play. (The word *computer* is written on the other side of the finish line to indicate that playing on the computer is allowed if the child stays on track and is ready early.)

Example of a Stay-on-Track Map for **going on a shopping trip.**

The goal in this plan is for a shopping trip to be a pleasant time for both parent and the Child. (The word *snack* is written on the other side of the finish line to indicate that a snack will be allowed at the end of the trip if the child stays on track throughout the shopping trip)

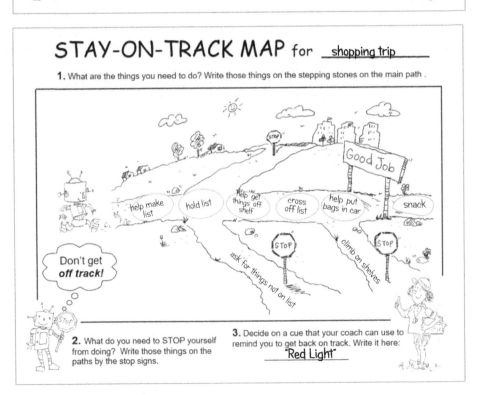

STAY-ON-TRACK MAP for ___morning___

1. What are the things you need to do? Write those things on the stepping stones on the main path.

Good Job

get dressed — breakfast — brush teeth — comb hair — make bed — computer

Don't get **off track!**

STOP — go outside — STOP

screen time

2. What do you need to STOP yourself from doing? Write those things on the paths by the stop signs.

3. Decide on a cue that your coach can use to remind you to get back on track. Write it here:
Are you on track?

STAY-ON-TRACK MAP for ___shopping trip___

1. What are the things you need to do? Write those things on the stepping stones on the main path.

Good Job

help make list — hold list — help get things off shelf — cross off list — help put bags in car — snack

Don't get **off track!**

STOP — STOP

ask for things not on list — climb on shelves

2. What do you need to STOP yourself from doing? Write those things on the paths by the stop signs.

3. Decide on a cue that your coach can use to remind you to get back on track. Write it here:
"Red Light"

STAY-ON-TRACK MAP for

1. What are the things you need to do? Write those things on the stepping stones on the main path.

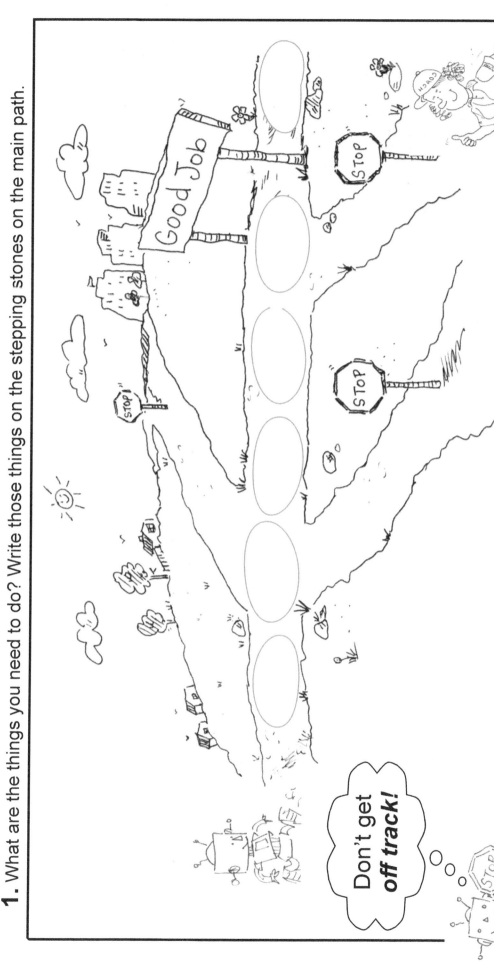

Good Job

STOP

STOP

STOP

Don't get **off track!**

STOP

2. What do you need to STOP yourself from doing? Write those things on the paths by the stop signs.

3. Decide on a cue that your coach can use to remind you to get back on track. Write it here:

Strategies for Success: Setting Goals

The objective of the Simon Says program is to help children learn to improve their performance in everyday situations. To achieve this, the child and family make a plan to take the knowledge and skills they have learned in therapy sessions and apply them to everyday life.

Using the **Coach's Report** and the child's **Things to Do** list, goals can be put in writing. The more specific the goals, the easier it will be for the child to succeed in transferring these skills to day-to-day challenges. Examples:

General goal: *Carlos will be good at the store.*

Specific goal #1: *Carlos will make a Stay-on-Track Map for the shopping trip.*

Specific goal #2: *Carlos and Mom will agree on a cue to help him if he gets off track.*

Specific goal #3: *Carlos will take the Map in the car and stay on track at the store.*

These can be written on the Coach's Report, the child's Things to Do list, or both:

COACHING TIP   Praise and encouragement can help children work hard toward goals. **Behavior-specific praise** is more effective than **general praise** because it reminds the child of the precise actions that led to success. Even if the child has experienced only partial success, highlighting what they did correctly can help build their confidence and motivate them to continue their efforts.

General praise: *You were good while I was cooking dinner tonight.*

Behavior-specific praise: *Carlos, I noticed that when you and Julia were playing the game, Julia didn't understand the rules and kept doing things wrong. I heard you start to yell at her, but then, when I gave you the cue, you stopped yourself and instead you explained the rules to her. I am really impressed that you remembered what we talked about and you stopped yourself and got back on track. I felt so happy to see that!*

Strategies for Success:
Recognition and Encouragement

In this section, the child learned about *response inhibition* and about its importance in everyday life. Practicing response inhibition can be very difficult for children with ADHD. As the child puts these concepts into practice, it is important to recognize even small steps in the right direction.

The *Yahoo!* materials in this section are one way to provide recognition and encouragement as the child tries out strategies and tools to improve response inhibition.

The **Yahoo!** materials include these tools:

You came up with a good plan to help us stay on track! Now we know what to *do* and what *not to do* while we are at the store.

1. For the coach: **Encouraging Words**

This page gives examples of encouraging statements that the coach can make at the "point of performance" to acknowledge the child's progress and to direct attention, in positive ways, to areas that still need some improvement. (The therapist can also add other, more specific, statements to fit the needs of a particular child. See examples of behavior-specific praise in the Coaching Tip box on the preceding page.)

Copy the Encouraging Words page and give it to the coach as a reminder.

2. For other caretakers: **Skill Tracker**

The *Skill Tracker* form provides a way for adults other than the coach to recognize and encourage effort and progress. The form includes a copy of the *Skills Checklist* for *response inhibition*, plus a specific goal that the child is working on. For example, while spending time with a family member, the child could practice responding to the cue *Red Light* as described in Assignment #2, Variation 1. Practicing response inhibition skills in a variety of contexts helps the child to recognize that response inhibition is a skill that can be practiced and improved.

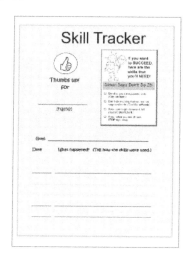

3. For the therapist: **Good Job! Tickets**

The therapist can provide additional incentive to complete assignments by awarding the child *Good Job!* Tickets. The tickets include the checklist of working memory skills that the child is working on, giving the therapist an opportunity to provide behavior-specific praise.

If desired, the therapist can have the child periodically "cash in" the tickets for a reward provided by the therapist. (Have a variety of rewards: inexpensive prizes and/or special activities to do at the office.)

In the *Simon Says* program, the coach:

- motivates the child by providing a vision of success

- creates interesting (and fun!) practice sessions

- sees that the child uses tools at the point of performance

- **recognizes even small signs of progress and provides encouragement**

If you want to SUCCEED, here are the skills that you'll NEED!

Simon Says Don't Do It!

- ❑ ***Do*** what you are supposed to do. (Stay ***on task.***)

- ❑ ***Don't do*** anything that you are not supposed to do. (Don't be ***off task.***)

- ❑ If you start to get distracted, tell Yourself, "***Don't Do It!***"

- ❑ If you notice you are off task, **STOP** right away.

As your child tries out strategies to support their **working memory**, this page gives examples of encouraging statements that you can make to point out areas of progress. You can also direct attention, in positive ways, to areas that still need some improvement.

Add other statements to fit the needs of your child, making the statements as specific as possible. In other words, don't just say *"Good job!"* Tell the child exactly what he/she did right, even if it is just a small detail. Believe that your child wants to succeed and help him/her build on each small step.

Encouraging Words

Getting started

You are stopping yourself as soon as you get the cue! I'm impressed!

We came up with a good plan to help us stay on track. Now we know exactly what **to do** and what **not to do.**

Troubleshooting

Let's practice stopping ourselves. Do you want to play Red Light/Green Light?

We got off to a good start with the Stay-on-Track Map. You had a hard time toward the finish. Next time, we'll have a shorter shopping trip. I think then you will be able to stay on track from start all the way to finish!

That didn't work out today, but we can try again. Let's work on the cue and see if we can make it "grab your attention" and remind you **why** you want to stay on track.

Recognizing effort and success

You are getting better at noticing when you are off-task. Good progress!

Nice way to get back on track. Now you are on your way to the finish line!

You stayed on track so well that now you have time to (play, watch TV, go outside, etc.)!

Skill Tracker

Thumbs up!
for

_____
(name)

If you want to SUCCEED, here are the skills that you'll NEED!

Simon Says *Don't Do It!*

❑ ***Do*** what you are supposed to do. (Stay ***on task.***)

❑ ***Don't do*** anything that you are not supposed to do. (Don't be ***off task.***)

❑ If you start to get distracted, tell Yourself, "***Don't Do It!***"

❑ If you notice you are off task, **STOP** right away.

Goal: _____

Date   What happened?   (Tell how the skills were used.)

_____   _____

_____   _____

_____   _____

_____   _____

- ❑ **Do** what you are supposed to do. (Stay **on task.**)
- ❑ **Don't do** anything that you are not supposed to do. (Don't be **off task.**)
- ❑ If you start to get distracted, tell yourself, "**Don't Do It!**"
- ❑ If you notice you are off task, **STOP** right away.

- ❑ **Do** what you are supposed to do. (Stay **on task.**)
- ❑ **Don't do** anything that you are not supposed to do. (Don't be **off task.**)
- ❑ If you start to get distracted, tell yourself, "**Don't Do It!**"
- ❑ If you notice you are off task, **STOP** right away.

- ❑ **Do** what you are supposed to do. (Stay **on task.**)
- ❑ **Don't do** anything that you are not supposed to do. (Don't be **off task.**)
- ❑ If you start to get distracted, tell yourself, "**Don't Do It!**"
- ❑ If you notice you are off task, **STOP** right away.

- ❑ **Do** what you are supposed to do. (Stay **on task.**)
- ❑ **Don't do** anything that you are not supposed to do. (Don't be **off task.**)
- ❑ If you start to get distracted, tell yourself, "**Don't Do It!**"
- ❑ If you notice you are off task, **STOP** right away.

Good Job! Tickets

Copy and cut on the dotted lines to make four tickets.

Use the tickets to reward and encourage the child's progress toward goals.

Put a checkmark by the skill (or skills) demonstrated and talk about the situation(s) in which it occurred.

This will help to raise the child's awareness of the specific behaviors that are helping him/her to succeed!

Summary
Don't Do It!

In this section children have learned about the importance of **stopping actions** that interfere with one's intentions or goals. They have been introduced to the idea of using private speech (internalized language) to inhibit responses that are counter-productive. They have also been introduced to the concept of self-monitoring (thinking about whether their behavior is off-task or on-task).

Before moving to the next section (*Cognitive and Behavioral Flexibility*) children should be fairly skilled at response inhibition. This ability to stop an ongoing response provides the foundation for monitoring–and regulating–their cognitive and physiological responses to upsetting circumstances.

Simon Says

Stop, Relax, Think

Help Kids Improve Their

Cognitive and Behavioral Flexibility

SECTION 3: *Stop, Relax, Think*
(Cognitive and Behavioral Flexibility)

Rationale for *Stop... Relax... Think* Activities

What is the problem?

Children with ADHD often have difficulty calming themselves down once they become excited or upset. They may also have difficulty with shifting gears or making transitions: stopping one activity (playing a video game) to begin another activity (getting ready for bed). These behaviors may cause difficulty in home, school, and social settings. Some children escalate and have "meltdowns" that are difficult for the parent or teacher to manage.

What executive functions are involved?.

The executive functions involved are those of:
- *Cognitive flexibility* – changing focus as the situation demands; shifting from agenda A to agenda B
- *Emotional control* – modulating one's emotional response appropriately to a situation or stressor
- *Internalized speech* – using self-talk to guide one's behavior and solve problems
- *Behavioral flexibility* – appropriately stopping one behavior and beginning a new behavior

How can we provide external support for working memory?

Children can:
1) practice specific skills involved in calming down and switching gears
   - deep breathing
   - muscle relaxation
   - positive "self-talk"
2) become more aware of the situations in which they most often need to use these skills
3) use a STOP sign as a visual cue to initiate the actions involved in calming down and switching gears

Remember: To be effective, support needs to be at the point of performance.

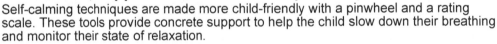

Self-calming techniques are made more child-friendly with a pinwheel and a rating scale. These tools provide concrete support to help the child slow down their breathing and monitor their state of relaxation.

Additional point of performance support is provided through the visual cue of a stop sign that is incorporated into a poster and a small cue card. Some children are eventually able to internally visualize a stop sign in stressful situations. But as always, the child should be given external support for as long as needed; the movement from external to internal control is different for each child.

Overview of *Stop, Relax, Think* Activities

	Activity or Assignment	Purpose	Page
STEP 1: **P**lay	STOP, Relax, Focus, *Go!*	Playing two different activities, the child learns to use **relaxation techniques** and **self-talk** as aids to switching from one activity to the next. A **STOP** sign is used as a **visual cue** to initiate these strategies.	99
STEP 2: **L**ink	Story: *The Team Player*	Sammy's soccer coach has taught him that, to be a **team player**, he has to sometimes make the switch from playing on the field to sitting on the bench. It's hard for Sammy to do, but he uses the team flag as a visual cue to initiate the self-calming and switching-focus techniques that he has learned.	103
	Worksheets	A review of the importance of switching focus in everyday life.	106
STEP 3: **A**ssign	Attention Please!	At home, the child practices switching focus in response to a cue from the coach. The child earns points on a score card.	113
	The Cool Down	Using the image of an alarmed cat and a cool-calm cat, the child practices paying attention to **body** and **breath** as a way to calm himself/herself.	117
	Stop and THINK Poster	The child makes a poster featuring a **STOP** sign which will serve as a cue to initiate **positive self-talk**.	121
	Stop and "B" Cool Cue Cards	The child is given a cue card to serve as a reminder to pay attention to the three "B"s: breath, body, and brain. The child uses the cue card to practice self-calming at home.	125
STEP 4: **Y**ahoo!	Encouraging Words Skill Trackers *Good Job!* Tickets	Adults provide feedback and encouragement as the child tries out new strategies and tools to improve cognitive and behavioral flexibility.	129

If you want to SUCCEED, here are the skills that you'll NEED!

STOP, Relax, Focus, *Go!*

❑ When you hear the cue, immediately **STOP** <u>all</u> action

❑ **RELAX** by paying attention to the 3 "B"s (breath, body, brain)

❑ **FOCUS** your mind by thinking about the new activity

❑ **SWITCH** to the new activity

Play Intervention:
STOP, Relax, Focus, *Go!*

In the play activity that follows, players are required to switch between two different games. In preparation for the activity, the child learns to use **relaxation techniques** and **self-talk** as an aid to switching focus. A *STOP* sign is used as a **visual cue** to initiate these strategies.

Begin by giving the child a copy of the checklist on this page. The checklist explains what the child needs to do to succeed at playing **STOP, Relax, Focus, Go!** Go over the checklist with the child *before* playing the game and use it again to review *after* playing the game.

The purpose of the game is to show children that they can already perform these skills in the context of play. In the steps following this **Play** activity (Link, Assign, and Yahoo!) the child and coach will learn strategies and tools that will help the child perform these skills in other contexts in day-to-day life.

If you want to SUCCEED, here are the skills that you'll NEED!

STOP, Relax, Focus, *Go!*

❑ When you hear the cue, immediately **STOP** <u>all</u> action

❑ **RELAX** by paying attention to the 3 "B"s (breath, body, brain)

❑ **FOCUS** your mind by thinking about the new activity

❑ **SWITCH** to the new activity

If you want to SUCCEED, here are the skills that you'll NEED!

STOP, Relax, Focus, *Go!*

❑ When you hear the cue, immediately **STOP** <u>all</u> action

❑ **RELAX** by paying attention to the 3 "B"s (breath, body, brain)

❑ **FOCUS** your mind by thinking about the new activity

❑ **SWITCH** to the new activity

STOP, Relax, Focus, *Go!*

Materials:

1. A STOP sign (You can purchase a STOP sign at an educational supply store, make your own, or use the one on page 123.)

2. The Skills Checklist on the preceding page.

3. Materials for two different ball games*:
  - a soft ball to throw;
  - a "basket" or container in which to throw the ball;
  - a writing board or piece of paper for recording names and scores.
  (Or materials for two other games: see **Variation***, below)

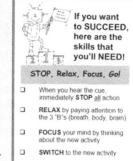

Get Ready: Prepare for this activity by teaching the child relaxation techniques. Tell the child:

In today's activity you have to be able to switch your focus, (or "switch gears"). That means you quickly and completely **STOP** *one game and* **get ready** *to start another.*

- *Quickly* *means that you stop the first game as soon as you get the signal to stop.*
- *Completely* *means that you won't even think about that first game anymore. You'll focus* **all** *of your attention on the new game. Even if you were having fun with the first game, you'll just "let go" of it and focus on the new game.*

It's not always easy to let go of something we want, so to help us make the switch, we are going use this **STOP** *sign as a reminder of how to "switch gears." You can use three things to help you switch, and the three things all start with the letter "B".*

- *You can use your* **Breath***:*
  When we take a deep breath, that helps us calm down and get ready to focus on something new.
- *You can use your* **Body***:*
  When we pay attention to our muscles and relax any that are tight or tense, that helps us get ready to focus.
- *You can use your* **Brain***:*
  We can talk to ourselves and say things that help us to calm down and focus.

Let's practice.
  First*, let's just look at the STOP sign*
    (Do all of these steps along with the child.)
  Next*, let's take a good, long, deep breath.*
    (Model this for the child.)
  Next*, let's pay attention to our bodies and relax any muscles that feel tight or tense.*
    (Model this for the child.)
  And last–*but not least*–*let's make sure our brains are sending us the right message.*
  I'm going to have my brain say. "Calm down. Get ready to focus on the new game."
  What are you going to have your brain say?

Continued next page

*Variation: In the instructions on the next page, the players switch between two different **ball games**. However, you can use any two games or activities that have high appeal for the child.

STOP, Relax, Focus, *Go!* (Continued)

Get Set: Tell the child:

> Today's activity is **STOP, Relax, Focus, Go!** We have to switch between two different games:
>> Game 1: **The Ball Toss Game** and
>> Game 2: **The First Annual World Championship Indoor Nerf Basketball Game.**
>
> For the **Ball Toss Game**, we just toss the ball back and forth, like this. But for the **First Annual World Championship Basketball Game**, we become world-famous NBA basketball players. Let's decide who we want to be, and I'll write our names on this Official World Championship Game Scoreboard.
>
>> Decide on names, giving the child help if needed. Write both names on the board.
>
> When we're world-famous NBA players, we try to throw the ball in the Official Game Goal. When we make it, we get a point on the score board. Let's each take a practice shot now.
>
> OK, here's how we play **STOP, Relax, Focus, Go!**
> • We start with **Game 1**–just tossing the ball back and forth.
> • Whenever I say **STOP**, we have to switch to **Game 2** and become our basketball players.
> • We'll make the switch by doing what we practiced. We will look at the STOP sign and
>> 1. take a deep **B**reath,
>> 2. relax the muscles in our **B**odies, and
>> 3. have our **B**rains focus our thinking on the new game.

Go:

(Note: The therapist should fully demonstrate all the steps below, and also model *internalized speech* by "thinking aloud" as they go through each step.)

If you want to SUCCEED, here are the skills that you'll NEED!

STOP, Relax, Focus, *Go!*

❑   When you hear the cue, immediately **STOP** all action

❑   **RELAX** by paying attention to the 3 "B"s (breath, body, brain)

❑   **FOCUS** your mind by thinking about the new activity

❑   **SWITCH** to the new activity

1. Begin with **Game 1** (just tossing the ball back and forth).
2. When the therapist says **STOP**, the player with the ball stops tossing the ball and focuses on a bright red **STOP** sign on the wall.
   (Internalized speech: *I'm stopping the Ball Toss Game. I am looking at the STOP sign and I'm not even going to think about the Ball Toss Game any more.*)
3. When the therapist says, "**Relax**," the player takes a deep breath and relaxes his/her body.
   (Internalized speech: *I'm taking a slow, deep breath to get ready for the new game. I'm checking my body to make sure I'm relaxed and ready to focus on the new game.*)
4. When the therapist says **Focus**, the player turns to the "basketball goal" and focuses his/her eyes and mind on the new activity.
   (Internalized speech: *I'm thinking just about the new game now. I'm focusing on being a basketball player and doing my best.*)
5. When the therapist says, "**Go!**," the player throws the ball to the basket.
   (Internalized speech: *"I made it!"* or *"I didn't make it, but that was a good effort." "I'm getting a little better each time." "I'll have another chance in a little while,"* etc.)
6. The player's score is recorded, and then the *Ball Toss Game* resumes until the therapist calls **STOP**.

Continue for several rounds. Make it fun, but be sure to emphasize the steps involved in switching focus: *stopping on cue, relaxing completely,* and *focusing thoughts on the new activity*.

Review: To review, go over checklist.

Play

Self-Talk: A Mental Tool

Internalized language, or **self-talk,** is a powerful mental tool that children can use
1) to help them stay calm and
2) to direct their own behavior.

Research shows that children who are inattentive and impulsive may have difficulty using effective self-talk. The **STOP, Relax, Focus, Go!** game introduces the idea of paying attention to what one is thinking and choosing positive ways of thinking.

The name of the game itself can become a positive message that children can say to themselves when agitated or upset: *"I'm going to stop, relax, and think"* or *"I'm going to stop, relax, and focus."*

COACHING TIP

Make this story come alive!

The story on the next page is written so that it can be read aloud as a "play."

There are three parts in this story. They are:
1) **Narrator**
2) **Sammy**
3) **Coach**

To make the parts easier to read, make a copy of the story for each reader. On each copy, highlight the part(s) to be performed by that reader.

Have fun!

If you want to SUCCEED, here are the skills that you'll NEED!

STOP, Relax, Focus, Go!

- ❏ When you hear the cue, immediately **STOP** <u>all</u> action
- ❏ **RELAX** by paying attention to the 3 "B"s (breath, body, brain)
- ❏ **FOCUS** your mind by thinking about the new activity
- ❏ **SWITCH** to the new activity

When do people use these skills in Real Life?

Sammy's soccer coach has taught him that, to be a "team player," he has to sometimes make the switch from playing on the field to sitting on the bench. It's hard for Sammy to do, but he uses the team flag as a visual cue to initiate the self-calming and "switching focus" techniques that he has learned.

The Team Player

Narrator: In the middle of the first half of the game, Coach gave Sammy the signal to come out of the game. Sammy didn't want to, but he headed for the bench anyway. Sammy felt so upset that he kicked the bench–*hard*–before he sat down. He thought to himself:

Sammy: *It's not fair! I was just about to score a goal.*

Narrator: Sammy tried to watch the game, but his mind was still focused on wanting to play the game. Sammy clenched his fists, kicked the water jug, and thought to himself:

Sammy: *Coach should have let me stay in! I know I can score a goal for the Hot Shots!*

Narrator: Coach saw Sammy kick the jug. He looked Sammy straight in the eye but he didn't say anything. He just pointed to the team flag. Then Coach turned his attention back to the game. Sammy looked at the flag and remembered what Coach always said: *"To be a team player you have to know when to switch gears."* That meant that sometimes Sammy had to SWITCH from playing on the field to watching from the bench. Sammy kept his eyes on the flag and did what Coach had taught him to do. He told himself:

Sammy: *It's time to switch gears. I'm going to STOP thinking about staying in the game, I'm going to RELAX.*

Narrator: Sammy took a big, deep breath and then let his breath out very, very slowly. He looked down at this clenched fists, took another breath, and relaxed his hands as he let out his breath. Then he took another deep breath and looked back at the flag. Next, he really FOCUSED his mind on what he needed to do for his team. He thought to himself:

Sammy: *I want to do the right thing. The other players have to have turns, too. My job now is to rest and to pay attention to the game.*

Narrator: When Sammy SWITCHED his attention to the field and to what the other players were doing, he felt a lot better. He also paid attention to what he was thinking. If he started to think:

Sammy: *It's not fair!*

Narrator: ...he STOPPED and told himself:

Sammy: *STOP! Be a team player!*

Narrator: ...and called out to support his team mates. With his full attention on the game, Sammy had a good time. When Doug made a great pass, Sammy cheered for him. When Jes missed the goal, he shouted:

Sammy: That's OK, you'll have another chance!

Narrator: The Hot Shots were playing a fierce game, but the competition was tough. By the middle of the second half, the players on the field were hot and worn down. Sammy felt a touch on his shoulder. He turned around. It was Coach.

Coach: Sammy, we need you in the game. The players on the field are tired and having a tough time. I've been watching you. When I called you off the field, you switched gears just like you were supposed to. You've been paying attention to the game and you are calm and relaxed. You're fresh and ready to go.

Sammy: I'm ready Coach!

Coach: In a minute, I am going to put you in at left forward. You have to stay in position, and focus on playing and on helping your teammates. Be positive, be patient, and your chance to score will come.

Sammy: OK Coach, I can do that.

Narrator: Sammy looked at the team flag. He shook his arms and legs and then stretched. He took some deep breaths and said to himself,

Sammy: *RELAX. Calm down. You can do it.*

Narrator: Sammy stood on the sidelines and focused his attention on Coach. He waited for him to give the signal. Then he ran on the field and joined his teammates. He remembered what Coach had told him to do. He stayed in position. He encouraged his teammates. Someone on the sideline made an ugly comment, but Sammy ignored it. He kept his eyes and ears focused on the game.

With just one minute left in the game, one of his teammates passed the ball to Sammy. It landed right in front of Sammy. His foot connected with the ball, and the ball found the net in the back of the goal. The Hot Shots were the tournament champs! The crowd went wild. Sammy's teammates crowded around him. Then Coach called the team together.

Coach: I'm really proud of all of you. We're going to celebrate our victory by going out for pizza. So let's pack up the gear and go!

Narrator: Sammy pulled the team flag out of the ground, put it in its bag, and carried it to Coach's truck. He handed it to Coach and said:

Sammy: I really like our flag. It helped me focus on the right thing today.

Coach: You're a real team player, Sammy. I really like *that*. Now let's go focus on eating pizza!

The Team Player

Questions for Discussion

How did Sammy feel when Coach gave him the signal to leave the field?

What did Sammy do to **switch** from playing on the field to watching from the sidelines?

What did Coach mean when he said "Be a team player?"

Sammy had to make another switch in the game. What was it?

Extra Questions

Think about the skills that you used when you played *STOP, Relax, Focus, Go!* In this story, which of those skills did Sammy use?

Sammy had to make the switch from playing the game to watching the game and cheering for his teammates. Tell about a time that you had to switch from one thing to another.

What do you think Coach thought to himself when he saw that Sammy had made the switch?

What do you think would have happened if Sammy had stayed upset and angry about having to switch?

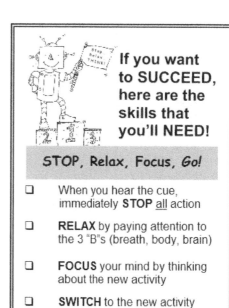

If you want to SUCCEED, here are the skills that you'll NEED!

STOP, Relax, Focus, *Go!*

❑ When you hear the cue, immediately **STOP** <u>all</u> action

❑ **RELAX** by paying attention to the 3 "B"s (breath, body, brain)

❑ **FOCUS** your mind by thinking about the new activity

❑ **SWITCH** to the new activity

Shifting Focus
In the story, Sammy uses the term "switch gears" to signify the skills needed to shift from agenda A to agenda B. Children may want to use that term or come up with their own term.

If you want to SUCCEED, here are the skills that you'll NEED!

STOP, Relax, Focus, *Go!*

❑ When you hear the cue, immediately **STOP** <u>all</u> action

❑ **RELAX** by paying attention to the 3 Bs (breath, body, brain)

❑ **FOCUS** your mind by thinking about the new activity

❑ **SWITCH** to the new activity

When do people use these skills in Real Life?

Move from Column A to Column B. Tell what the person can do to switch from A to B.

A	CUE	STOP	RELAX	FOCUS	B
PERSON **Here is what they are doing NOW.**	This is the cue that tells them it is time to switch gears.	What do they have to STOP doing?	**Show** how they can use their breath and bodies to get ready to switch.	What should they **think** in order to focus on the new activity?	**GO!** **This is the new activity that they have to switch to.**
Father: is having a bad day at work, his boss yelled at him, and he is feeling angry	Clock says 5:00; work day is done				**Pick up his child and take him to baseball practice**
Teacher: is in the break room with other teachers, laughing, joking and having fun	Bell rings; break is over				**Go to important meeting with the principal**
Child: is lying in bed, half-asleep	Alarm clock rings				**Get on the school bus**
Coach: is losing the game, 5-1	Referee's whistle; game is over				**Have dinner with his family**

If you want to SUCCEED, here are the skills that you'll NEED!

STOP, Relax, Focus, Go!

- ❑ When you hear the cue, immediately **STOP** <u>all</u> action
- ❑ **RELAX** by paying attention to the 3 Bs (breath, body, brain)
- ❑ **FOCUS** your mind by thinking about the new activity
- ❑ **SWITCH** to the new activity

Link

When do people use these skills in Real Life?

How about <u>YOU</u>?

When do you need to use these skills in Real Life?

At SCHOOL,

it is easy for me to switch from

_____ to _____

it is hard for me to switch from

_____ to _____

One thing that I could do to help myself "switch gears" is

_____

At HOME,

it is easy for me to switch from

_____ to _____

it is hard for me to switch from

_____ to _____

One thing that I could do to help myself "switch gears" is

_____

Point of Performance and the Coach's Role

Because of the importance of using interventions at the **point of performance**, the role of the "coach" is an integral part of the *Simon Says Pay Attention* program. At home, a parent or other adult can act as coach. In a school setting, a teacher or other staff member can act as coach at the point of performance.

Using the Coach's Report

It is important to have good communication between the therapist and the coach, so that therapist can make adjustments to the program based on the particular needs of the child and the family (and/or classroom).
The coach's report on the next page provides a concise way to keep the therapist and coach "on the same page" as the child progresses through the Simon Says program.

- We recommend that the therapist introduce the use of the **Coach's Report** during the **Link** activities and continue to use the reports as part of the **Assign** activities.

- The therapist can help the child and coach formulate goals during the therapy session, writing them directly on the **Coach's Report.**

- The **Coach's Report** can then go home with the coach at the end of each session.

- At the next session, the coach returns the completed form to the therapist prior to the start of the session.

- In addition to showing the progress the child has made on the goals, the report will update the therapist on any significant events that have occurred since the last session and any special concerns that need to be addressed.

The **Coach's Report** on the opposite page is specific for Part 3 of the Simon Says program. Use the *Don't Do It!* checklist to help formulate goals that are related to **switching focus.**

It can be a huge challenge for children to work on becoming more flexible in their thoughts and behavior. Initially, create goals to help children just increase their awareness of the need to shift focus or shift gears.

Goal: Find two examples of times you switched focus and did well.

Goal: Find two examples of times it was hard switch focus.

COACH'S REPORT   Date_____

Child's Name _____

Coach's Name _____

If you want to SUCCEED, here are the skills that you'll NEED!

STOP, Relax, Focus, Go!

☐ When you hear the cue, immediately **STOP** <u>all</u> action

☐ **RELAX** by paying attention to the 3 "B"s (breath, body, brain)

☐ **FOCUS** your mind by thinking about the new activity

☐ **SWITCH** to the new activity

1) Please list any significant events that have occurred since your child's last therapy session:

....

....

....

....

2) Brief description of your child's behavior, mood, etc., in the past week:

....

....

....

3) Do you have any specific concerns or questions today?

....

....

....

4) Progress toward goals

Goal: _____

Very Dissatisfied	Dissatisfied	Neutral - Unsure	Satisfied	Very Satisfied
-2	-1	0	1	2

Goal: _____

Very Dissatisfied	Dissatisfied	Neutral - Unsure	Satisfied	Very Satisfied
-2	-1	0	1	2

Goal: _____

Very Dissatisfied	Dissatisfied	Neutral - Unsure	Satisfied	Very Satisfied
-2	-1	0	1	2

Comments on goals:

....

....

....

Things to Do:

Name: _____

Date: _____

If you want to SUCCEED, here are the skills that you'll NEED!

STOP, Relax, Focus, Go!

❏   When you hear the cue, immediately **STOP** <u>all</u> action

❏   **RELAX** by paying attention to the 3 "B"s (breath, body, brain)

❏   **FOCUS** your mind by thinking about the new activity

❏   **SWITCH** to the new activity

REMEMBER:

You've got the skills that you need to succeed!

Assign

Attention, Please!

Sarah, it's time for bed...... Class, put away your spelling and take out your math..
These are everyday **cues**, signaling that it is time to "make a change." Giving a
parent or teacher **full attention** will help the child prepare for making
the change. In our culture, giving someone full
attention includes demonstrating the appropriate "body
language." Not all children learn this intuitively.
Demonstration and practice can help a child develop
the habit of stopping and giving full attention in
preparation for a switch of focus.

Page 113

The Cool Down

To be successful with self-calming, children need to be aware of how their bodies
react when they become upset. This activity helps them
learn to deepen their breathing and relax their muscles.
It shows that self-calming is a skill that can be
practiced and improved.

Page 117

Stop and THINK Poster

With the previous assignment (*The Cool Down*) the child
practiced deep breathing and muscle relaxation.
This assignment focuses on the third skill:
self-talk to guide behavior.

Page 121

STOP and "B" Cool Cue Cards

The previous assignments focused on the skills needed for self
calming and switching focus. This activity gives the child the
opportunity to practice these skills in real-life situations.
   1. A pocket sized cue-card will serve as a visual reminder
   of the strategies involved in calming down.

   2. The child will also select a cue that others can use
   to alert him to the need to calm himself down.

Page 125

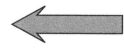 Use the **Things to Do** list to give the child a written reminder of the assignment.

COACHING TIP

PRACTICE, PRACTICE, PRACTICE!

Before beginning the **Attention, Please!** assignment, practice in the therapist's office.

Practice not only the child's response to the cue, but also the coach's response to the child's behavior.

Also practice how to mark the score card. *Emphasize that if the child does not always score a point, that is OK.* The purpose of the assignment is for the coach to help the child improve the skill. The coach should **show** the child how to improve their response and remind the child that they will have lots more chances to score a point.

Assignment Idea #1:
Attention, Please!

Executive Functions
- Shifting Focus
- Emotional Control
- Internalized speech
- Inhibiting Behavior
- Initiating Behavior

RATIONALE: *Sarah, it's time for bed...... Class, put away your spelling and take out your math..* These are everyday **cues**, signaling that it is time to "make a change." Giving a parent or teacher ***full attention*** will help the child prepare for making the change. In our culture, giving someone full attention includes demonstrating the appropriate "body language." Not all children learn this intuitively. Demonstration and practice can help a child develop the habit of stopping and giving full attention in preparation for a switch of focus.

BENEFIT: In this assignment, the coach gives a **cue** that means the child should STOP what he/she is doing and give the coach full attention, in preparation for a change of focus The child then practices taking the correct action, including appropriate body language. The coach gives immediate feedback to help the child improve, as needed.

MATERIALS NEEDED:

1. ***Attention Please!* Cue Cards** (Copy and cut out the three cards on the next page. Fold each in half. The cue card will be the front; the score card will be the back. Tape along sides.)
2. Copy of the checklist for the ***STOP, Relax, Focus, Go!*** activity
3. Copy of the instructions for the coach to take home

EXPLANATION FOR CHILD:
Review checklist for the *STOP, Relax, Focus, Go!* activity.
Remind the child of his/her success and say:

> *In this assignment, you'll practice those same skills at home and you'll get to earn points. You'll have 10 practice sessions, so you can earn up to 10 points. You'll know it's time for a practice session when your coach gives you the cue. The cue is* Attention Please! *You will* **hear** *the cue word when your coach says it, and you'll also* **see** *the cue word on this cue card.*

Demonstrate all parts of the Attention, Please! assignment.

1st, demonstrate the coach's job: have the cue card and pencil in hand and say, *"Attention Please!"*

2nd, demonstrate the child's job, pretending to be absorbed in playing a game or watching TV and then taking the right action by:
   1) Stopping what you are doing
      (Explain what this means–turning off the TV, putting down the game.)
   2) Showing with your body language that you are listening
      (Demonstrate both appropriate and inappropriate body language.)
   3) Listening quietly for what your coach will say next
      (Demonstrate giving good eye contact and remaining silent.)
   4) Responding to what your coach says or asks.
      (Demonstrate responding to a simple instruction such as, *"Please put this book on the desk."*)

Have the child demonstrate those 4 actions.

3rd, demonstrate the coach's job of completing the score card. Comment on what the child has done. For example:

> *You stopped playing with the ball when you heard the cue, "Attention, Please!" You turned around and looked right at me and waited patiently. You listened and heard what I asked you to do. You did what I asked you to do. Great job of listening and switching focus! Now I am going to give you a check on the score card.*

113

ASSIGNMENT (continued):

Give the coach three **Attention, Please!** cards. Discuss with the coach how to use the cards in the child's daily life:

1. Talk about what to say to the child once the child gives the coach full attention. Emphasize the importance of keeping the practice session fun by mixing this up. For example the coach can:

   - Give the child a simple thing to do (Please feed the dog.)

   - Ask a question (Do you want cheese on your hamburger?)

   - Give an unexpected surprise (Would you like to help me make cookies?)

   - Give your child a hug and say, "I just wanted to say *I love you!*"

   - Give a compliment ("I like when you play so nicely with your little brother.")

2. Decide on a **start date** and an **end date** for the assignment. Write these on the first of the three score cards.

3. It may be helpful for the family to complete one card and bring it back to the therapist before using the other two cards. The therapist can help make adjustments if there are any difficulties in implementing the assignments.

4. To get the maximum value from this assignment, use all three cards. However, this assignment can be very enjoyable, so many children want to repeat it often.

COACHING TIP

EARNING POINTS: You may be surprised by how much children enjoy this simple activity. Part of the charm, from the child's point of view, is the challenge of earning points. In deciding how the child can redeem the points earned, keep it simple! Some ideas: make cookies or popcorn together, read a book of riddles together, do an art project together, play croquet, or create the menu for dinner one night. Write each idea on a piece of paper and put them in a cup. If they earn x number of points, they can pick an activity out of the cup. It's the ritual and the recognition that are important, not the elaborateness of the reward!

Copy the three cards. Cut them out and then fold on the dotted line to create a two-sided card. Tape along the sides.

Attention, Please!
Score Card

Start Date _____   End Date_____

1 ___   2 ___   3 ___   4 ___   5 ___
6 ___   7 ___   8 ___   9 ___   10___

√ = correct response to cue

O = incorrect response to cue

Attention, Please!
Score Card

Start Date _____   End Date_____

1 ___   2 ___   3 ___   4 ___   5 ___
6 ___   7 ___   8 ___   9 ___   10___

√ = correct response to cue

O = incorrect response to cue

Attention, Please!
Score Card

Start Date _____   End Date_____

1 ___   2 ___   3 ___   4 ___   5 ___
6 ___   7 ___   8 ___   9 ___   10___

√ = correct response to cue

O = incorrect response to cue

COACHING TIP

In practicing these self-calming strategies at home, begin by practicing at a neutral time such as bedtime. This allows the child to gain confidence and lays a foundation for the child to later use the same strategies under more stressful circumstances.

The therapist may want to provide a chart for the child to record practice sessions (and also consider providing some sort of reward for completing the chart).

When stressful circumstances arise, the child may need a reminder (or cue) to use the strategies that he or she has learned. But the more often the strategies have been practiced at neutral times, the easier it will be to implement them under stressful situations.

Assignment Idea #2:
The Cool-Down

Executive Functions
- Shifting Focus
- Emotional Control
- Internalized speech
- Inhibiting Behavior
- Initiating Behavior

RATIONALE: Many children have difficulty with being flexible, both in their thinking and in their behavior. For example, they may resist transitioning form one activity (or idea) to the next, or have difficulty calming themselves down if they become upset. To be successful with transitioning and self-calming, children need to be aware of how their bodies react when they become upset. This activity helps them learn to slow and deepen their breathing and relax their muscles in preparation for thinking differently about what is happening.

BENEFIT: This activity helps to **raise children's awareness** that self-calming is a skill that can be practiced and improved. In this activity children:
- practice concrete strategies to slow and deepen their breathing and relax their muscles.
- use a tool for self-monitoring, *The Cool-Down Rating Scale.*

MATERIALS NEEDED:
1. A small pinwheel
2. The *Cool-Down Rating Scale* (page 119)
3. A digital timer (or a watch or clock with a second hand)

EXPLANATION FOR CHILD:

Everyone gets upset from time to time. Even animals get upset. And when we get upset, our bodies react. Think of a cat when it sees a big, barking dog. First, the cat's brain sends an alarm: Something is wrong!

When its body gets that alarm, the cat arches its back and extends its claws. And it hisses. The cat's body is ready to do something–to either fight the dog or to run away from the dog. Let's pretend we are cats and our brains have sent an alarm. Let's show our something-is-wrong reactions.

Show the picture of the alarmed cat on the rating scale. With the child, practice acting out the cat's reactions.

Today, every time I say, "Something is wrong!" that will be our cue to pretend to be cats that see a big barking dog.

Together with the child, act out the cat's something-is-wrong reaction again.
Then, do this quickly each time you say, "something-is-wrong," during the explanation below. Have fun with this!

Although acting like something is wrong is a good thing when there is danger, a cat doesn't want to go around arching its back and hissing all the time. So, as soon as a cat knows that it is safe, it does the Cool-Down. Just as quick as can be, it switches from a something-is-wrong cat to a cool-calm cat.

A something-is-wrong cat is ready to fight but a cool-calm cat is ready to play with a toy or to curl up and take a catnap. It stretches it's body. It yawns and takes a deep breath. Then it stretches its body one more time. Let's practice switching from a something-is-wrong cat to a cool-calm cat.

Practice switching from tense muscles and hissing to stretching, relaxing and breathing deeply. Point to the picture of the relaxed cat on the rating scale. Praise the child for being able to switch from upset to calm.

(Continued on next page.)

NOTE: Younger children may want to pretend to be a cat–over and over. If so, allow the child to have fun pretending to be a cat, but emphasize the skill that the child displays in switching:
- *You are a cat who knows how to really **stretch** your muscles and **relax**.*
- *Look at this cool cat! It takes a deep, deep breath all the way down to its tummy.*
- *This cat knows how to slow down and get ready for a nice long cat-nap.*

THE COOL-DOWN (continued)

After completing the play activity, tell the child:

Your assignment is to practice at home so that you can get really, really good at making the switch from upset to calm. To do that you need to pay close attention to three things:

   1st - slow down your breath

   2nd - relax your muscles

   3rd - check yourself to see how relaxed you are

DEEP BREATHING

1st, let's practice breathing. We'll use this pinwheel to help us. We will each take a deeeep breath and then let it out slooooowly. When we breathe out, let's see how long we can keep the pinwheel moving. The deeper and slower we breathe, the longer we'll be able to keep the pinwheel going.

Alterative #1 - Use bubbles instead of a pinwheel :
When we breathe out, let's see if we can make a big bubble and not burst it.

Alterative #2 - Use a "pretend candle" instead of bubbles:
Put your finger in front of your mouth and pretend it's a candle. Pretend that there is a flame and when we breathe out, we want to make the flame move and flicker, but we don't want to blow it out. So, we have to let our breath out very slowly and gently.

Practice this several times. If desired, make it more challenging by timing the length of the out-breath, using a digital timer or a watch with a second hand. Once the child has shown success at deep breathing, move on to the next step (which also involves a deep exhalation of breath):

MUSCLE RELAXATION

Now, *let's learn to relax our bodies by stretching and releasing our muscles. We are going to make "Air Angels*
- Put your hands (palms together) in front of your stomach.

- Slowly, raise your hands straight above your head (your ears will be between your arms).

- Standing on tip-toes, stretch your whole body up as tall as you can.

- Hold that tight, tight. Make your muscles very tense.

- Now let's try to stretch and tighten up a little bit more. Stay like that and hold your breath.

- Now, sloooowly lower your arms to your sides, like fluffy angel's wings.

- As you slowly bring down your arms and let your hands fall to your sides, breathe slowly

   out, and let your muscles switch from tense to relaxed.

- Pay attention and notice how it feels as you let your whole body relax and become calm.

Practice this several times. Make sure that the child really feels the difference between the **tension** with arms an body outstretched and the **release** of muscles and breath.

SELF-MONITORING

After doing this a time or two, introduce the concept of *self-monitoring,* using the *Cool Down Rating Scale* (see next page).

Let's do this one more time and this time we are going to check how relaxed we are and rate ourselves.

Show the child the rating scale and demonstrate how to use it. Initially, do not use a rating of "1" (the most relaxed) when you evaluate yourself; model improving your performance.

Next, give the child the rating scale and have the child demonstrate. Make adjustments or give suggestions as needed.

Finally give the child their own copy of the rating scale (and a pinwheel if available) and tell the child:

Practice your deep breathing and muscle relaxation at home. Use the Cool-Down Rating Scale to check how well you are doing. Next time we'll practice together again.

Cool Down Rating Scales
Copy on heavy paper and cut out to make three rating scales.

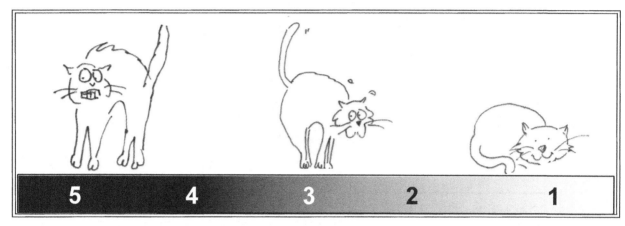

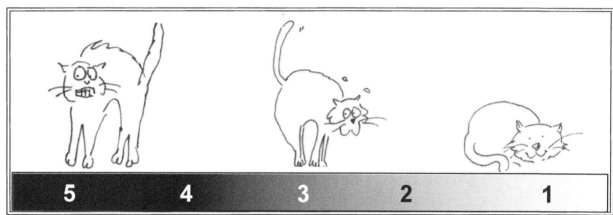

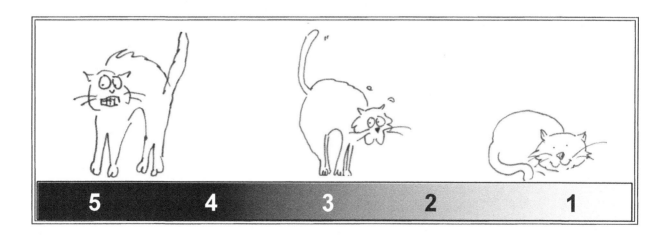

COACHING TIP

COACH'S ROLE: The coach can remind the child to:
- practice using the ***Stop and THINK* Poster** and
- give praise for the child's effort. (See Encouraging Words, *Getting Started* section on page 130.)

As with the previous assignment, practicing at a neutral time such as bed time allows the child to gain confidence in using the skills and prepares the child for using the skills under more stressful circumstances. In the next assignment, the child will put all of these skills together and use them in real-life situations.

Assignment Idea #3:
Stop and THINK Poster

Executive Functions
- Shifting Focus
- Emotional Control
- Internalized speech
- Inhibiting Behavior
- Initiating Behavior

RATIONALE: To be successful with self-calming and switching focus, children need to have skills in three areas:
1. slow breathing,
2. muscle relaxation and
3. self talk to guide behavior.

BENEFIT: With the previous assignment (*The Cool Down*) the child practiced deep breathing and muscle relaxation. This assignment focuses on the third skill: ***self-talk to guide behavior.***

MATERIALS NEEDED:
1. A STOP sign poster (Page 123)
2. Optional: small pictures to decorate the poster (clip art, magazine photos, or pictures drawn by the child)

EXPLANATION FOR CHILD:

First, review the story, *The Team Player*, in which Sammy uses the team flag as a cue to "switch gears."

*You have been learning a lot about how to switch gears. With the Cool-Down Assignment, you practiced breathing and relaxing. Sammy did both of those things to help him switch gears, and he also did something else. He paid attention to what he was thinking. If he started feeling upset or thinking angry thoughts, he told himself, "STOP." He reminded himself those thoughts and feelings were **false alarms**. Instead, he told himself things that helped him calm down and focus on the game. Some of the things that he told himself were:*

Relax   **You can do it**
I want to do the right thing   **It's time to switch gears**
Be a team player   **Calm down**

Can you think of other things that people tell themselves to help themselves calm down and focus on the right thing? (Count to ten, Take a deep breath, etc.)

ASSIGNMENT:
Your assignment is to make a Stop and THINK *poster. Your poster will have:*

1. A STOP sign. When Sammy looked at the flag, it was a **cue**. It reminded him to STOP thinking angry thoughts and to start telling himself things that would help him calm down.

2. Words to calm yourself and think about the best thing to do. In the bubbles around the STOP sign, write some things that you can tell yourself. You can use the same words Sammy did or you can think of your own, or use some of his and some of your own.

3. Pictures. If you'd like, you can also add pictures that will remind you of what to tell yourself.

After you have made your poster, put it with your pinwheel and Cool-Down Rating Scale. When you practice your cool-down, look at your STOP sign and read the words you have written.

COACHING TIP

The Stop and THINK poster can be used in any situation in which the child has difficulty coping. For example, if your child hates doing homework, help your child be aware of his or her "self-talk" about homework. Start with the statements that you have heard your child say out loud. Then dig a little deeper, asking *"What are you saying to yourself inside your head?"* (See examples in the first column, below. It may help to give examples of things you have said to yourself in a similar situation.)

Discuss how your child feels with these thoughts in mind (discouraged, frustrated, etc.) Remind your child that, if we change the way we *think* about the situation, we can change the way we *feel*, which in turn helps us to *act* differently. Help your child brainstorm for more helpful thoughts (*"thoughts that help you feel more encouraged and hopeful"*) and write those on the poster.

Review the poster before beginning homework. Add more helpful thoughts and revise the poster occasionally, as needed. It may take a while for your child to identify the most helpful thoughts and form a habit of using the poster as external support.

1. Help your child figure out what thoughts go through their head at homework time:

I want to watch TV first.

It's too much. I'll never get it done.

I wish I could be playing outside with my friends.

Mom is so mean. she won't let me play.

Maybe I can go to a different school.

I want to finish that video game I was playing.

I wonder who will win the soccer game tomorrow?

Jamie gets to play. I wish I were still in Kindergarten.

2. Help your child brainstorm: *What are the most helpful things to tell yourself about homework?*

If I want to play outside I need to start right away.

I can do the work. It's not too hard.

If I stick with it and get it all done, Mom will let me watch TV.

I'll use the timer to help me work faster.

I'm a hard worker. I can do this!

If I get this done on time, I am going to feel HAPPY!

3. Have your child write the helpful thoughts on the poster:

123

COACHING TIP

Remind your child that in the story, ***The Team Player***, Sammy doesn't realize at first that his brain is sending him a false alarm. But his coach does, so he gives Sammy a cue. See if your child recalls what the cue is (Coach points to the flag) and what Sammy does when he gets the cue. (He takes a deep breath, uses positive self-talk, etc.)

Let your child know that everyone from time to time has the same problem as Sammy—we may not realize that our brain is sending us a false alarm. So, it can be helpful to have someone like Sammy's coach to give us a cue so we can do the right thing, just as Sammy did. Discuss with your child the benefits to Sammy when his coach is attentive and gives him a cue.

After your child has practiced the skills for **Stop and B Cool**, suggest that the two of you set up a cue to use in case, like Sammy, your child's brain "sends a false alarm." If a situation arises and you give a cue and your child ignores the cue, be patient. Wait until things have calmed and then have this discussion again. Have your child commit to trying again and practice, this time role-playing some-one starting to get upset and then responding to a cue. (Your child may enjoy switching roles around and giving *you* the cue!)

Assignment Idea #4:
Stop and "B" Cool Cue Cards

Executive Functions
- Shifting Focus
- Emotional Control
- Internalized speech
- Inhibiting Behavior
- Initiating Behavior

RATIONALE: To be successful with strategies for switching focus, children need to practice in real-life situations.

BENEFIT: The previous assignments focused on the skills needed for self-calming and switching focus. This activity gives the child visual, external support in using those skills in real-life situations.
1. A pocket sized cue-card will serve as a visual reminder of the strategies involved in calming down.
2. The child will also select a cue that others can use to alert the child to the need to use calming strategies they have learned.

MATERIALS NEEDED:
The **STOP and "B" Cool** picture (page 126) and a cue card (page 127)

EXPLANATION FOR CHILD:

Review *The Cool-Down* assignment on page 117. Stress that, when the brain sends the message, *"Something is wrong!,"* the body automatically responds.)

People have the same kind of "Something is wrong!" reaction that cats do. In the story, The Team Player, when Sammy has to leave the field, his brain sends him an alarm: "It's not fair!" And as soon as his brain sends that alarm, his body reacts: he clenches his fist, he makes a face, he kicks the water jug. His body is getting ready to fight.

Now, we know that it is a false alarm. There is no reason for Sammy to fight. He'll have a chance to play again later. In fact, getting ready to fight could make things worse. If Coach sees that Sammy is upset, he might decide not to put him back in the game.

Fortunately, when Coach points to the flag, Sammy figures out that he has sent himself a false alarm. So he uses his 3 "B's"–his Breath, Body, and Brain–to switch gears.

Use the STOP and "B" Cool picture (page 126) to review the three things that Sammy does to cool down.

ASSIGNMENT:

"Switching gears" is a skill that we all need. Some days, it may seem that our brains react to every little thing and send us lots of false alarms. If we don't figure out that it is a false alarm, like Sammy did, we may not cool down. Your assignment is to notice a time when your brain gives you a false alarm and then use the 3 "B's" to calm yourself down. This card can remind you of the things you need to do to calm down and make a good choice.

Give the child a copy of the *STOP and "B" Cool* cue card.
Give an extra copy or two to the coach. (It may be helpful to keep several in strategic locations.)
Have the child come up with a cue that the coach can use as a reminder, if needed.

PRACTICE: **Role-play what is expected. Be sure the child takes enough time with each step:**
1. **Something upsetting happens to the child,**
2. **leading to an initial, upset reaction, then**
3. **use of a card to cue the child's calming-down skills.**

Also, role-play a situation in which the child needs to get a reminder from the coach, using the cue they decided on.
Switch roles, if desired, giving the child a chance to give the cue.

and "B" Cool

Breath:
Take a
slow and **deep**
breath

Body:
Relax
your muscles

I can make
the right choice.

Brain:
Focus on
the right
message

Stop and "B" Cool Cue Cards

1. Copy this page on heavy paper
2. Cut out the three cards
3. Fold each card in the middle (along the dotted line)
4. Tape the edges to make a 2-sided card
5. Laminate if possible

COACH'S ROLE:
The coach will play a critical role in this assignment. Go over the *Encouraging Words* on page 130, especially the "Troubleshooting" section. Look for small signs of progress and keep improving.

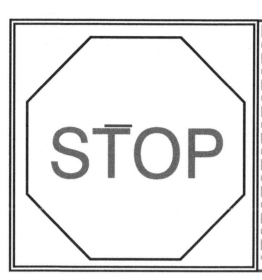

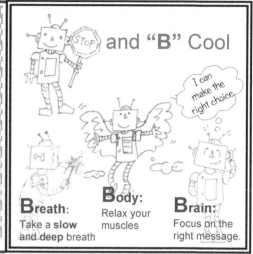

THERAPIST'S ROLE:
This assignment requires a lot of effort on the part of the child. It may be helpful if the therapist details the assignment in writing and provides *Good Job! Tickets* (page 132) for completion of this assignment.

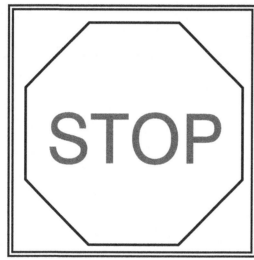

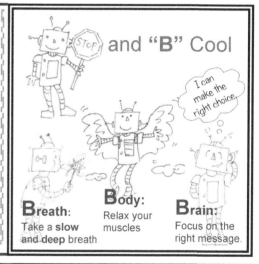

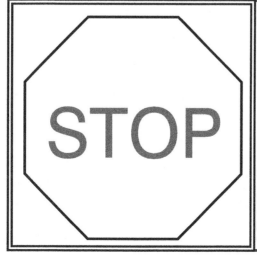

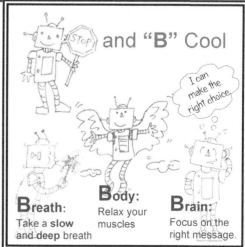

Strategies for Success: Setting Goals

The objective of the Simon Says program is to help children learn to improve their performance in everyday situations To achieve this, the child and family make a plan to take the knowledge and skills they have learned in therapy sessions and apply them to everyday life.

Using the **Coach's Report** and the child's **Things to Do** list, goals can be put in writing. The more specific the goals, the easier it will be for the child to succeed in transferring these skills to day-to-day challenges. Examples:

General goal: *Kylie will follow instructions in the classroom.*

Specific goal #1: *Kylie will practice "Attention, Please!" with her counselor at school.*

Specific goal #2: *On Monday, Kylie will bring her teacher an "Attention, Please!" card.*

Specific goal #3: *By Friday, Kylie will have at least 6 checks on her card.*

These can be written on the Coach's Report, the child's Things to Do list, or both:

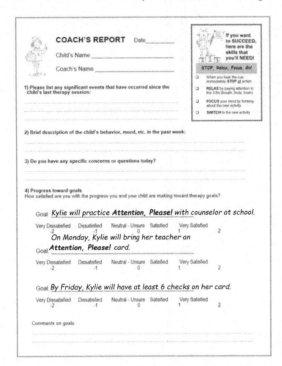

COACHING TIP

Praise and encouragement can help children work hard toward goals. **Behavior-specific praise** is more effective than **general praise** because it reminds the child of the precise actions that led to success. Even if the child has experienced only partial success, highlighting what they did correctly can help build their confidence and motivate them to continue their effort.

General praise: *You were good in class today, Kylie. You didn't fuss.*

Behavior-specific praise: *Kylie, you got frustrated with the work that you had to do. But when I pointed to the Stop and "B" Cool card on your desk, you remembered what to do. You took a deep breath and got yourself calm. And you got the work done pretty quickly! What did you say to yourself to help yourself stay on track?*

Strategies for Success: Recognition and Encouragement

In this section, the child learns about **switching focus** (cognitive and behavioral flexibility) and practices strategies for self-monitoring and self-calming. These are complex and difficult behaviors: first, stopping oneself from initiating one's automatic or impulsive response to a situation, AND second, calming down and shifting focus The more the child practices these strategies in non-stressful contexts, the easier it will be to apply those skills in situations where the child becomes emotionally upset. The coach and therapist should work closely together to encourage the child to practice using strategies and tools that support his or her ability to switch focus.

The **Yahoo!** materials in this section are one way to provide that recognition and encouragement as the child tries out strategies and tools to improve cognitive and behavioral flexibility.

> Great job of shifting gears. I'm impressed with how you stuck with it!

The **Yahoo!** materials include these tools:

1. For the coach: **Encouraging Words**

This page gives examples of encouraging statements that the coach can make at the "point of performance" to acknowledge the child's progress and to direct attention, in positive ways, to areas that still need some improvement. (The therapist can also add other, more specific, statements to fit the needs of a particular child. See examples of behavior-specific praise in the Coaching Tip box on the preceding page.)

Copy the Encouraging Words page and give it to the coach as a reminder.

2. For other caretakers: **Skill Tracker**

The **Skill Tracker** form provides a way for adults other than the coach to recognize and encourage effort and progress. For example, let's imagine that the child has difficulty switching focus at dance or karate class. Fill in the child's name and a goal (**"When reminded, Noah will use the Cool-Down Rating Scale to get calm and focused."**) The coach can briefly explain how the rating scale works and ask the teacher to use the cue **"It's time to use your rating scale."**

After class the teacher, if willing, could complete the form. If this isn't feasible, the coach can gather the information from the teacher and complete the form.

3. For the therapist: **Good Job! Tickets**

The therapist can provide additional incentive to complete assignments by awarding the child Good Job! Tickets. The tickets include the checklist of working memory skills that the child is working on, giving the therapist an opportunity to provide behavior-specific praise.

If desired, the therapist can have the child periodically "cash in" the tickets for a reward provided by the therapist. (Have a variety of rewards: inexpensive prizes and/or special activities to do at the office.)

In the *Simon Says* program, the coach:

- motivates the child by providing a vision of success.

- creates interesting (and fun!) practice sessions.

- sees that the child uses tools at the point of performance.

- **recognizes even small signs of progress and provides encouragement.**

As your child tries out strategies to support their **working memory**, this page gives examples of encouraging statements that you can make to point out areas of progress. You can also direct attention, in positive ways, to areas that still need some improvement.

Add other statements to fit the needs of your child, making the statements as specific as possible. In other words, don't just say *"Good job!"* Tell the child exactly what they did right, even if it is just a small detail. Believe that your child wants to succeed and help them build on each small step.

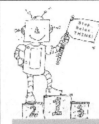

If you want to SUCCEED, here are the skills that you'll NEED!

STOP, Relax, Focus, Go!

- ❑   When you hear the cue, immediately **STOP** <u>all</u> action

- ❑   **RELAX** by paying attention to the 3 "B"s (breath, body, brain)

- ❑   **FOCUS** your mind by thinking about the new activity

- ❑   **SWITCH** to the new activity

Encouraging Words

Getting started

You responded perfectly when I gave you the "Attention, Please!" cue.

Let's practice those cool-down skills. You can show me how.

Troubleshooting

It's not easy to switch gears when you are very upset. Perhaps I waited too late to give you the cue. I'll try to do better next time. And perhaps we need to make the cue stronger, so it will really "grab" your attention.

I know that your intentions are good. Sometimes, when we get frustrated, we forget our good intentions. Let's think hard about **why** you want to (get your homework done/be nice to your sister, etc.) Let's make your intentions bigger and stronger than your frustrations.

Recognizing effort and success

Your Stop & THINK poster has some great ideas on it. Let's make another poster and put it in a spot where all of us can use it. We can all practice being careful thinkers!

You are taking time to practice with your pinwheel, rating scale and poster. That 's going to pay off.

Great job of shifting gears. That's not easy. I'm impressed with how you stuck with it.

Thanks for cooling down. I could see you taking a deep breath and relaxing your body.

Skill Tracker

Thumbs up!
for

_____

(name)

If you want to SUCCEED, here are the skills that you'll NEED!

STOP, Relax, Focus, Go!

❑ When you hear the cue, immediately **STOP** <u>all</u> action

❑ **RELAX** by paying attention to the 3 "B"s (breath, body, brain)

❑ **FOCUS** your mind by thinking about the new activity

❑ **SWITCH** to the new activity

Goal: _____

Date   What happened? (Tell how the skills were used.)

_____ _____

_____ _____

_____ _____

_____ _____

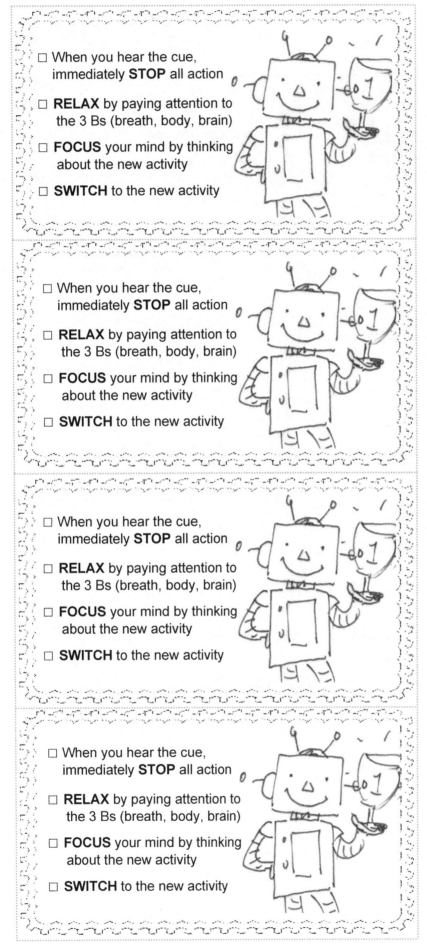

- ☐ When you hear the cue, immediately **STOP** all action
- ☐ **RELAX** by paying attention to the 3 Bs (breath, body, brain)
- ☐ **FOCUS** your mind by thinking about the new activity
- ☐ **SWITCH** to the new activity

- ☐ When you hear the cue, immediately **STOP** all action
- ☐ **RELAX** by paying attention to the 3 Bs (breath, body, brain)
- ☐ **FOCUS** your mind by thinking about the new activity
- ☐ **SWITCH** to the new activity

- ☐ When you hear the cue, immediately **STOP** all action
- ☐ **RELAX** by paying attention to the 3 Bs (breath, body, brain)
- ☐ **FOCUS** your mind by thinking about the new activity
- ☐ **SWITCH** to the new activity

- ☐ When you hear the cue, immediately **STOP** all action
- ☐ **RELAX** by paying attention to the 3 Bs (breath, body, brain)
- ☐ **FOCUS** your mind by thinking about the new activity
- ☐ **SWITCH** to the new activity

Good Job! Tickets

Copy and cut on the dotted lines to make four tickets.

Use the tickets to reward and encourage the child's progress toward goals.

Put a checkmark by the skill (or skills) demonstrated and talk about the situation(s) in which it occurred.

This will help to raise the child's awareness of the specific behaviors that are helping them to succeed!

Summary
Stop, Relax, Think

In this section, children have learned about the importance of sometimes **stopping** their automatic or impulsive response to a situation in order to calm themselves, monitor their reactions, and make adjustments as appropriate to the situation. They have learned to pay attention to their "brains" (their self-talk or internalized language) as an important component in self-regulation.

In the next section (*Goal Orientation*), the child will need to draw upon all of the previously learned skills, plus learn new strategies for planning and time management. Self-talk will continue to be emphasized as a means to motivate oneself and follow a plan in a timely manner.

Simon says
I've Got a Plan!

Help Kids Improve Their
Goal Orientation

SECTION 4: I've Got a Plan!
(Goal Orientation)

Rationale for *I've Got a Plan!* Activities

What is the problem?

Lack of organization, poor sense of time, and difficulty following through on a task are characteristics of ADHD. A child told to clean his room may be off to a good start until he finds the toy that grandma sent for his birthday. Then he remembers that he forgot to send a thank you note and wanders off to the kitchen in search of pencil and paper. He finds his baseball cards in the kitchen drawer and sits down at the table and begins to divide them into teams. When his mom yells at him five minutes later, he is truly puzzled as to why she is upset.

What Executive Functions are involved?

The executive functions involved include:
- *Goal orientation* - establishing an image of the goal in one's mind for the purpose of completing a task or activity
- *Planning & organizing* - developing steps ahead of time, establishing order in an activity or space, and carrying out a task in a systematic matter
- *Working memory* - recalling all of the steps that need to be completed
- *Sense of time* - keeping track of the passage of time; altering behavior in relation to time
- *Self-monitoring* - checking one's progress to assure attainment of a goal

How can we provide external support for working memory?

Children can:
1) learn to create a **visual game plan** as a way to externalize the executive functions involved in goal orientation
2) play games that can help them better understand their **sense of time**
3) use positive self-talk to "reward" and motivate themselves as they monitor their progress

Remember: To be effective, cues need to be at the point of performance.

Because of weaknesses in executive function, children with ADHD need to have sufficient external support at the point of performance.

The visual "game plan" at the point of performance helps the child keep in mind the steps to be taken and also supports self-monitoring by allowing the child to mark and visualize progress towards completion. The *Encouraging Words* Cue Cards provide support for effective self-talk at the point of performance.

Overview of *I've Got a Plan!* Activities

	Activity or Assignment	**Purpose**	Page
STEP 1: **P**lay	The *I've Got a Plan!* Game Show	As a contestant on a "game show," the child plans steps–and tracks progress–in working towards a goal. This activity introduces the idea of using a **visual game plan** as an aid to goal orientation. Each contestant is also assigned a "time manager" and a "coach," reflecting the executive functions of *sense of time* and *monitoring and motivation.*	139
STEP 2: **L**ink	Story: **Have Fun, Get the Job Done**	Abby is overwhelmed by the task of cleaning her room. She thinks she'll never get it done in time to visit her friend. Abby's grandmother uses a game board to help map out a visual plan that breaks the job into smaller steps and gives Abby a way to track progress toward her goal.	143
	Worksheets	A review of the importance of goal orientation in everyday life.	146
STEP 3: **A**ssign	Make-Your-Own Game Plan	The child makes a **game plan** as an external guide to 1) planning steps toward a goal and 2) tracking progress toward a goal.	153
	Encouraging Words **C**ue Cards	The child uses positive self-talk as a way to 1) motivate himself/herself	157
	Beat the Clock!	To help the child become more aware of the passage of time, the child practices guessing how much time is needed to complete a particular action or activity.	163
STEP 4: **Y**ahoo!	Encouraging Words Skill Trackers *Good Job!* Tickets	Adults provide feedback and encouragement as the child tries out new strategies and tools to improve planning, self-monitoring and time management.	165

If you want to SUCCEED, here are the skills that you'll NEED!

I've Got a Plan!

❑ Make a **PLAN** to get all of the parts done.

❑ Choose a way to **TRACK** your progress.

❑ **FOCUS** on one part at a time.

❑ When you finish one part, mark your progress and **SWITCH** to the next part.

❑ When you finish all the parts, give yourself a big **"Yahoo!"**

Play Intervention:
I've Got a Plan!

As a contestant on a "game show," the child plans the steps needed to complete a goal. This activity introduces the idea of using a **visual game plan** as an aid to **goal orientation**.

Each contestant is also assigned a "time manager" and a "coach" reflecting the executive functions of *sense of time* and *self-monitoring*.

Begin by giving the child a copy of the checklist on this page. The checklist explains what the child needs to do to succeed at playing *I've Got a Plan*. Go over the checklist with the child *before* playing the game and use it again to review *after* playing the game.

The purpose of the game is to let the child realize that he already has these skills.

In the steps following this **P**lay activity (**L**ink, **A**ssign, and **Y**ahoo!) the child and coach will learn strategies and tools that will help the child be able perform these skills when and where they are needed in day-to-day life.

If you want to SUCCEED, here are the skills that you'll NEED!

I've Got a Plan!

❑ Make a **PLAN** to get all of the parts done.

❑ Choose a way to **TRACK** your progress.

❑ **FOCUS** on one part at a time.

❑ When you finish one part, mark your progress and **SWITCH** to the next part.

❑ When you finish all the parts, give yourself a big **"Yahoo!"**

If you want to SUCCEED, here are the skills that you'll NEED!

I've Got a Plan!

❑ Make a **PLAN** to get all of the parts done.

❑ Choose a way to **TRACK** your progress.

❑ **FOCUS** on one part at a time.

❑ When you finish one part, mark your progress and **SWITCH** to the next part.

❑ When you finish all the parts, give yourself a big **"Yahoo!"**

The **I've Got a Plan!** Game Show

Special Note: This activity calls for three participants in addition to the contestant: 1) the game show host, 2) the time manager, and 3) the coach. If needed, once person can double up and fill two roles. **Also,** define one part of the room to be the "stage" for the Game Show.

Materials:

1. Four (or more) pre-selected "challenges." (See list of suggestions below.)
2. A copy of **I've Got a Plan!** (Page 141)
3. A game board marker. (It's fun to have an assortment to choose from.)
4. A timer.
5. A copy of the skills checklist on the preceding page.

Some possible "challenges"
- Put together a small puzzle
- String beads in a color pattern
- Line up dominoes
- Build a structure with blocks
- Complete a simple maze or crossword puzzle
- Sort items by color
- Sort cards by suit
- Make an animal with playdough

Each task should be developmentally appropriate for the child, fun to do, and simple enough to be completed in about **one minute**. If needed, scale down the difficulty of the task (such as the dominoes, beads, cards) by including fewer items.

Get Ready: **Prepare the child to be the contestant on the show**

1. *Welcome to the* **I've Got a Plan! Game Show**. *In just a few minutes, you'll be our first contestant.*
   *All contestants must set themselves a **goal** of completing four challenges.*
   The Game Show Host–that's me–will select the four challenges for each contestant.
   *Then the contestant–that's you–has to make a **Game Plan** to show how you'll reach your goal.*
      Give the child a copy of I've Got a Plan!, but don't go over it yet.
   Finally, you have to complete all four parts of the Game Plan in eight* minutes.
   We'll go over your job in a few minutes, but first, let's meet your helpers.

   > * Vary the time limit according to child's abilities; be sure to provide more than enough time to get all of the challenges completed.

2. *Each contestant has two helpers.** Let's go over their jobs next.*
   *You have a **time manager**, to help you keep track of how much time has passed*
      Make sure that the time manager has a timer. Talk about how important this job is, because the contestant not only needs to complete all four challenges, they have to complete them *on time*. The time manager should let the contestant know how much time is remaining. (5 minutes left; 4 minutes left, etc.)

   *And you have a **coach**, to keep you on track and encourage you to do your best.*
      Give the coach a set of the *Encouraging Words Cue Cards* (page 158-159.) Spend some time talking about how important it is for the contestant to stay on track. Encouraging words can motivate you to stay on track or to get back on track if you get off track. Look over the cards and discuss what the coach might say when the contestant is on track. What might the coach say as a "cue" if the contestants gets off track?
   Your coach is also in charge of leading us all in a big, "Yahoo!" when you reach your goal. Let's all practice the "Yahoo!" part–make it nice and loud!
      Have fun with this part–ham it up!

   > ** The reason for including the two helpers is to **externalize** functions (*time management* and *self-monitoring*) that you will want the child to eventually learn how to do on their own. Later in this section, there will be Assignments related to these functions. (**Encouraging Words** for self-monitoring and **Beat the Clock** for time management.)

3. *OK, contestant, before the show starts, I'll show you the four challenges that I've selected for you.*
      Show the four challenges and explain what is required for each.
      Then set the four challenges on a chair ("the challenge chair") or at another other spot some distance away from the "stage" where the contestant will perform the challenges.

Get Set: The show begins...

Game Show Host: *Welcome to the* I've Got a Plan! Game Show. *Our first contestant today is* _____. *Contestant, step right up. Let's see if you have the skills that you'll need to succeed. Let's look at our* I've Got a Plan! *checklist.*

Show the Skills Checklist. Read it over once, quickly.

Now, contestant, let's go over these one by one and see if you've got what it takes.

The 1st skill *on the list is to map out a* **GAME PLAN** *for meeting your goal.*

Put the copy of *I've Got a Plan!* **on a writing surface.**

There are four blank spaces on the game plan, one for each challenge. You decide which challenge you want to do first, and write that in the first blank space on the game plan.

Continue and have the child complete all 4 parts. Point out that the 3rd space shows that it is time to take a quick break (take a breath, stretch, do some jumping jacks, etc.)

The 2nd skill *is to keep* **TRACK** *of your progress. Choose a marker and put it on the START space.*

Have the child choose a marker (playing piece) and put it on the Start space.

Leave your marker there until it is time to do the first challenge. When I say, "GO," move you marker to the first space, see what is written on it, and go to the "challenge chair" and get that challenge.

Demonstrate moving the marker to the 1st space.

The 3rd skill *is to* **FOCUS** *your attention on the part that you are working on.*

Keep working at each part until you get it done. Don't worry about the time. Your Time Manager will let you know how you are doing on your time.

Have the Time Manager take a bow.

> **Note:** If the child forgets to move the marker, the coach can give a reminder:
> *"Check your plan."*
> *"Move your marker."*

The 4th skill *is to* **SWITCH**.

After you finish one challenge, move your marker to the next space, read what is says, and go and get that challenge from the "challenge chair."

Demonstrate moving the marker to the 2nd space.

This space in the middle is for you to take a small break. Check with your Coach to see how you are doing.

Have the Coach take a bow.

If you want, you can take some deep breaths or do some jumping jacks. Then get back on track. When you have finished all parts of your challenge, you will move your marker to **FINISH**.

Demonstrate moving the marker along the path to the FINISH.

The last skill *is to reward yourself a big* **"Yahoo!"** *just like we practiced.*

Go:

- Begin by reminding the child to move the marker as soon as you say *"Go!"* Then say, *"Ready, Set, Go!"*

- Keep it fun by commenting to the "studio audience" about the progress the contestant is making in following the *Game Plan* and about the help the contestant is receiving from the Time *Manager* and the *Coach*, etc.

- Remember, the purpose of this activity is to give the child practice in creating and using a visual "game plan." Use the game plan terminology as much as possible: (*Our contestant is checking his plan to see what the next step is. ... Our contestant is moving to the next step on his plan. ... Right now our contestant is focusing on the 4th part of his plan. ... The Time Manager and the Coach are keeping our contestant on track toward the Finish.*)

- Don't forget the big *"Yahoo!"* when the child completes the challenges and moves to the Finish space.

Review: Use the checklist to REVIEW the skills demonstrated.

COACHING TIP

Make this story come alive!

The story on the next page is written so that it can be read aloud as a "play."

There are three parts in this story. They are:
   1) **Narrator**
   2) **Abby**
   3) **Grandmother**

To make the parts easier to read, make a copy of the story for each reader. On each copy, highlight the part(s) to be performed by that reader.

Have fun!

 Link

If you want to SUCCEED, here are the skills that you'll NEED!

I've Got a Plan

☐ Make a **PLAN** to get all of the parts done.

☐ Choose a way to **TRACK** your progress.

☐ **FOCUS** on one part at a time.

☐ When you finish one part, mark your progress and **SWITCH** to the next part.

☐ When you finish all the parts, give yourself a big *Yahoo!*

When do people use these skills in Real Life?

Abby is overwhelmed by the task of cleaning her room and thinks she'll never get it done in time to visit her friend. Abby's grandmother uses a game board to help map out a visual plan that breaks the job into smaller steps and gives Abby a way to track her progress toward her goal.

HAVE FUN, GET THE JOB DONE

Narrator: Abby was excited. Her neighbor, Mia, had just called and invited her go to the park for a picnic. If Abby could go, Mia and her parents would be there at 11:30 to pick her up. Abby hung up the phone and ran to her grandmother.

Abby: Guess what? Mia invited me to go to the park for a picnic! Can I go?

Grandmother: That sounds like fun! And it's a perfect day for a trip to the park. But don't forget that your mom said you have to clean your room before you leave the house.

Narrator: Abby groaned. She had forgotten about cleaning her room. All of a sudden, she didn't feel so happy.

Abby: Do I have to? *Please* let me do it when I get back. I'll never get it done by 11:30.

Grandmother: It's only 10:00. You have plenty of time.

Abby: I hate to clean my room. It's too hard!

Grandmother: Let's take a look at that room.

Narrator: When Abby opened the door to her room, it looked even worse than she had remembered. There were dirty clothes everywhere. Her science project was spread out on her desk, along with parts of her coin collection. All of her games were on the floor. And even though she couldn't see them, she knew that there were candy wrappers and old drawing papers under the dirty clothes and games.

Abby: See what I mean? It will take me all day to clean up this mess!

Grandmother: I agree, it is a mess.

Abby: Will you help me? Please? Otherwise I'll never get it done in time!

Grandmother: I am just agreeing that it's a mess. I'm not agreeing that you can't get it done on time. And you don't need my help. You just need some help from a few things that I see lying around on your floor

Narrator: Abby looked at the floor, wondering what her grandmother could be thinking. Her grandmother picked up one of the game boards. It had a space that said, "**Start Here**," another that said "**Finish-*You win!*"** and a path between those two spaces

Abby: Are we going to play a game?

Grandmother: No, we are going to make a *game plan*.

Narrator: Abby's grandmother explained that a game plan helps you get a job done on time. She handed Abby the board and pointed to the space that said **Finish - *You win!***

Grandmother: Your goal is to get your room clean by 11:30, right?

Abby: Right, so I can go with Mia.

Narrator: Grandmother went to the desk and found a pencil and some sticky-notes. She wrote 11:30 one of the notes and stuck if on the game board by the **Finish - *You win!*** space. Then she wrote 10:00 on another sticky-note.

Grandmother: You are starting now, and it's 10:00. So I wrote 10:00 on this one. I'll put it by the space that says **Start.** Now we have to figure out how to get you from Start to Finish.

Narrator: She handed Abby the pad of notes. Then she told Abby to think of all the things she needed to do to get her room cleaned. She told her to write one thing–just one thing–on each note.

Abby: I have to take my dirty clothes to the laundry room and put away all my games.

Narrator: Abby wrote dirty clothes on one note and games on another. She gave the notes to her grandmother and her grandmother put them on the path after the Start space.

Abby: And I have to put away my coin collection and straighten out all my science project stuff.

Narrator: Abby wrote coin and science project on two notes. Her grandmother stuck those on the path. The path was filling up and there was just a little space left before the **Finish** space.

Grandmother: I can think of at least two other things you need to do.

Narrator: Abby looked around the room and saw the candy wrappers and drawing papers on the floor. She wrote sweep floor on a note and added that to the board.

Grandmother: Good job, Abby. There's one more thing I'm thinking of. I'll give you a hint. It rhymes with "bake your bread."

Narrator: Abby laughed and wrote make my bed on a note. She put that on the board. It looked like a game to play. Abby smiled.

Abby: That was fun!

Narrator: Her grandmother looked under some dirty socks and found a gameboard marker. She put it on the ***Start*** space.

Grandmother: This gameboad marker is **you.** If you just stay on track and move along this path, doing one task at a time you should have plenty of time to get your room clean and be ready by 11:30.

Narrator: Abby looked at the board. It gave her a different way to think about cleaning up her room. And it didn't seem so hard any more. She felt much better.

Abby: I think I can do it.

Grandmother: I'll get a timer and let you know how you are doing and how much time you have left. I'll be your cheerleader and cheer you all the way to the ***Finish*** line. And you'll win a trip to the park!

Narrator: Abby gave her grandmother a hug.

Abby: Thanks, Grandma, for making it **fun** to get the job **done.**

The Game Plan
Questions for Discussion

At the beginning of the story, why did Abby beg her grandmother to let her clean her room when she got back from the park?

How did Abby feel after she made the **Game Plan**? Why did she feel that way?

Tell about a time that another person helped you to make a good plan.

If you want to SUCCEED, here are the skills that you'll NEED!

I've Got a Plan

❏ Make a **PLAN** to get all of the parts done.

❏ Choose a way to **TRACK** your progress.

❏ **FOCUS** on one part at a time.

❏ When you finish one part, mark your progress and **SWITCH** to the next part.

❏ When you finish all the parts, give yourself a big *Yahoo!*

Extra Questions
Remember the skills that you needed to succeed when you played *I've Got a Plan!* Did Abby use some of those skills in her Game Plan? Which ones?

Creating a game plan "externalizes" a number of executive functions:

Goal Orientation: It was difficult for Abby to establish an internal image of her goal and an internal plan for reaching her goal. Creating a game plan helped her to "see" that the job was easier than she'd imagined it to be.

Planning & Organization: By putting the tasks on sticky-notes, Abby and her grandmother could physically manipulate the "steps" involved as an aid to planning.

Working Memory: By attaching the steps to the board, in the order to be completed, Abby created a sequential list of what to do next, providing external support for her working memory.

Sense of Time: A poor sense of time is central to the difficulties experienced by individuals with ADHD. Abby's grandmother offers external support for Abby's poor sense of time with a timer and reminders.

Self-monitoring: By moving a game marker along the path from start to finish, Abby has an external confirmation of her progress toward her goal. This confirmation will help her to regulate her level of interest and motivation and make it more likely that she will stick with the plan.

Note: Her grandmother's offer to be a "cheerleader" provides additional external support and will help to regulate Abby's level of motivation. Assignment Idea #2 (Encouraging Words Cue Cards) teaches children to be their own "cheerleaders" by using self-talk to regulate their level of motivation.

If you want to SUCCEED, here are the skills that you'll NEED!

I've Got a Plan

❑ Make a **PLAN** to get all of the parts done.

❑ Choose a way to **TRACK** your progress.

❑ **FOCUS** on one part at a time.

❑ When you finish one part, mark your progress and **SWITCH** to the next part.

❑ When you finish all the parts, give yourself a big *Yahoo!*

When do people use these skills in Real Life?

In the story, *Have Fun, Get the Job Done,* Abby set a goal, then planned the steps toward her goal. For each person listed below, help to think of some of the steps they will need to reach their goal.

Person & Goal	What are some of the steps the person must take to reach the goal?				Yahoo! What can the person say or do to congratulate themselves when they reach their goal?
Farmer: have 500 pumpkins ready for Halloween.					
Teacher: have students put on a play for parents.					
Baker: make a big cake for the wedding tomorrow.					

If you want to SUCCEED, here are the skills that you'll NEED!

I've Got a Plan

❏ Make a **PLAN** to get all of the parts done.

❏ Choose a way to **TRACK** your progress.

❏ **FOCUS** on one part at a time.

❏ When you finish one part, mark your progress and **SWITCH** to the next part.

❏ When you finish all the parts, give yourself a big *Yahoo!*

When do people use these skills in Real Life?

How about <u>YOU</u>?

When do you need to use these skills in Real Life?

1. Pretend that you are helping to plan a surprise birthday party for your grandmother. Think of four things you need to do to get ready for the party:

_____

_____

_____

_____

2. Pretend that your family is going to the beach for a vacation. Think of four things that your family needs to do to get ready for the vacation:

_____

_____

_____

_____

Point of Performance and the Coach's Role

Point of performance

Because of the importance of using interventions at the **point of performance**, the role of the "coach" is an integral part of the *Simon Says Pay Attention* program. At home, a parent or other adult can act as coach. In a school setting, a teacher or other staff member can act as coach at the point of performance.

Using the Coach's Report

It is important to have good communication between the therapist and the coach, so that the therapist can make adjustments to the program based on the particular needs of the child and the family (and/or classroom). The coach's report on the next page provides a concise way to keep the therapist and coach "on the same page" as the child progresses through the Simon Says program.

- We recommend that the therapist introduce the use of the **Coach's Report** during the **Link** activities and continue to use the reports as part of the **Assign** activities.

- The therapist can help the child and coach formulate goals during the therapy session, writing them directly on the **Coach's Report.**

- The **Coach's Report** can then go home with the coach at the end of each session.

- At the next session, the coach returns the completed form to the therapist prior to the start of the session.

- In addition to showing the progress the child has made on the goals, the report will update the therapist on any significant events that have occurred since the last session and any special concerns that need to be addressed.

The **Coach's Report** on the opposite page is specific for Section 4 of the Simon Says program. Use the *I've Got a Plan!* checklist to help formulate goals that are related to **goal orientation.**

You may want to begin with goals related to raising the child's awareness of how much difficulty they may have in formulating and/or following through on a plan. For example:

Goal: _Tell about a time it was hard to get something done on time._

Goal: _Tell about a time someone helped you follow a plan._

COACH'S REPORT   Date_____

Child's Name _____

Coach's Name _____

1) Please list any significant events that have occurred since your child's last therapy session:

....

....

....

....

2) Brief description of your child's behavior, mood, etc. in the past week:

....

....

....

3) Do you have any specific concerns or questions today?

....

....

....

4) Progress toward goals

Goal: _____

Very Dissatisfied	Dissatisfied	Neutral - Unsure	Satisfied	Very Satisfied
-2	-1	0	1	2

Goal: _____

Very Dissatisfied	Dissatisfied	Neutral - Unsure	Satisfied	Very Satisfied
-2	-1	0	1	2

Goal: _____

Very Dissatisfied	Dissatisfied	Neutral - Unsure	Satisfied	Very Satisfied
-2	-1	0	1	2

Comments on goals:

....

....

....

Things to Do:

Name: _____

Date: _____

If you want to SUCCEED, here are the skills that you'll NEED!

I've Got a Plan

- ☐ Make a **PLAN** to get all of the parts done.
- ☐ Choose a way to **TRACK** your progress.
- ☐ **FOCUS** on one part at a time.
- ☐ When you finish one part, mark your progress and **SWITCH** to the next part.
- ☐ When you finish all the parts, give yourself a big *Yahoo!*

_____

_____

_____

_____

_____

_____

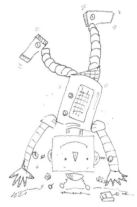

REMEMBER:

You've got the skills that you need to succeed!

Assign

Assignment Idea # 1

Make-Your-Own Game Plan

Children can learn to organize complex tasks, and monitor their progress by using a visual game plan, like the one used in the *I've Got a Plan!* **Game Show.** This activity helps to raise the child's awareness that achieving goals can be made easier if the overall job is broken down into a series of smaller steps, with a plan for when to do during each step.

Page 153

Assignment Idea # 2

Encouraging-Words Cue Cards

In the activity, *I've Got a Plan!,* the final skill that the child demonstrates is congratulating themselves on a job well done, by giving a big *"Yahoo!"* While this may not appear to be an important "skill," the ability to appreciate one's own progress provides a way to keep oneself motivated while working on tedious jobs that provide little in the way of immediate pay-off. This assignment teaches the child to use **positive statements** as a means of motivating oneself to complete a difficult task.

Page 157

Assignment Idea # 3

Beat the Clock!

Rationale: According to Russell Barkley, time is the "ultimate yet nearly invisible disability afflicting those with ADHD." This assignment is designed to help the child:
1) become more aware of the concept of the *passage of time*
2) practice estimating how much time is needed to complete a particular action or task or activity
3) regulate his or her actions in order to complete a set of actions within a specified period of time.

Page 161

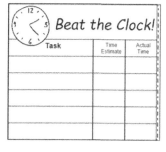

 Use the **Things to Do** list to give the child a written reminder of the assignment.

COACHING TIP

Use a ***Game Plan*** often and for different kinds of tasks and activities. With lots of practice using an *external* game plan, the child may begin to visualize an *internal* game plan to help organize and direct his or her behavior.

However, the child should continue to use an **external plan** for as long as needed. Even adults vary greatly in their need to externalize planning functions.

Assignment Idea #1:
Make-Your-Own Game Plan

Executive Functions
- Planning
- Working Memory
- Sense of Time
- Self-monitoring
- Goal Orientation

RATIONALE: Children can learn to organize complex tasks, and monitor their progress by using a visual game plan, like the one used in *I've Got a Plan!*

BENEFIT: This activity helps to **raise the child's awareness** that it is easier to achieve goals if the overall job is broken down into a series of smaller steps, with a plan for when to do each step

MATERIALS NEEDED:

1. A blank Game Plan. Use a pre-made one (see pages 141 or 154) or have the child compose one using the game board pieces on page 155. (Or use sticky notes, as Abby did in the story, *Have Fun, Get the Job Done.*)
2. A marker (game piece) to track progress.

ASSIGNMENT: The coach and child choose a job or activity for which they will create a game plan. It can be:
- a chore that is challenging for the child
- a big job for the family to do together
- a social event (for example, have a family movie night or go on a picnic.)

Pieces for Game Plan

Copy and cut out the pieces and assemble on paper. Add personal artwork to create a custom *Game Plan*. (The *Simon, Coach,* and *Good Job!* pieces can be used to take a break, check in with the coach, and/or give a *Yahoo!*)

COACHING TIP

Internalized language, or self-talk, is an important mental tool that helps us to organize our actions and stay on track. Research has shown that children with ADHD are slower to internalize helpful language. The ***Encouraging Words*** assignment helps children to be more aware of using positive self-talk. Some children may need more support than others in learning how to do this, so coach involvement is extremely important. That's why this assignment is done in two stages, with the coach choosing the cards initially before the child is expected to do so independently.

In addition to helping us organize and motivate our behavior, self-talk also helps us to regulate our emotions. If your child has difficulty regulating emotions, you may want to spend additional time on the Stop and B Cool assignment, asking the child to pay special attention to the "brain" –"*What can you tell yourself that will help you stay calm and make good choices?*"

Assignment Idea #2:
Encouraging-Words Cue Cards

Executive Functions
- Shifting Focus
- Emotional Control
- Internalized speech
- Inhibiting Behavior
- Initiating Behavior

RATIONALE: In the activity, *I've Got a Plan!*, the final skill that the child demonstrates is congratulating himself on a job well done by giving a big *"Yahoo!"* While this may not appear to be an important "skill," the ability to appreciate one's own progress provides a way to stay motivated while working on tedious jobs that provide little in the way of an immediate pay-off.

BENEFIT: This assignment teaches the child to use **positive statements** as a means of encouraging during the completion of a difficult task. The task can be anything that is difficult for the child to stick with: cleaning a room, washing the dishes, doing homework.

Note: If homework takes hours, don't try to apply this assignment to the entire homework process. Instead, pick one homework task–for example, writing spelling words–and use it with that. Then try with other non-homework tasks, then again later with homework. The goal is to teach the child a *skill*, so initially use situations where the child can experience success fairly easily. As the child becomes more skilled, the assignment can be applied to more challenging situations.

MATERIALS NEEDED: Copy and cut out the *Encouraging-Words* **Cue Cards** (pages 158-9)

EXPLANATION FOR CHILD:

Remember in I've Got a Plan! Game Show *you gave yourself a "Yahoo!" when you finished. It's good to congratulate ourselves when we succeed at something. Some jobs are harder than others, and for really hard jobs, it's a good idea to give ourselves lots of little "Yahoos" along the way and then one big "Yahoo" at the end of the job.*

In the I've Got a Plan! Game Show, *your coach helped you stay on track by praising you when you were doing well or by giving you a reminder if you got off track. In this activity, you are going to learn to be your own coach. You'll praise yourself when you stay on track. You'll give yourself a reminder if you get off track.*

ASSIGNMENT:

1) ***In the first stage***, another person acts as the coach and observes the child as he or she performs the task. The coach will provide positive statements and reminders to encourage the child and keep the child on track. However, rather than saying the statements aloud, they are given in the form of "cue cards." (Sample cue cards are provided on pages 158-159, or use index cards to make customized cue cards for the child.)

   As the child works on the task, the coach watches silently. Every minute or so, the coach provides the child with an appropriate cue card, either recognizing success or reminding the child–in a positive way–to stay on track. ***The child should then read the cue card aloud.***

2) ***In the second stage***, the child selects the cue cards. In this stage, the coach gives a **cue** (for example, ringing a bell.) When the child hears the cue, the child selects an appropriate cue card, either recognizing success or encouraging himself/herself to stay on-track. Here again, the child should read the card aloud.

DEMONSTRATE:

In the office, the therapist should demonstrate. Give the child a simple activity to complete. (See the list of challenges on page 139 for ideas). Have the child and coach practice both stages of the assignment. Allow about ten minutes for the activity with five minutes for the first stage and five minutes for the second stage.)

COACH'S ROLE: The coach should decide on a home-based task for using this assignment at home. (See note under "BENEFIT," above.)

I'm aiming high!

I can do it.

p trying!

Keep up the good work!

Don't give up!

I'm on track to reach my goal

I need to check my plan.

Take some deep breaths

I've got a winning attitude.

Remember: A good attitude counts!

I'll reach my goal soon!

Good Job!

I can do it!

I'm working hard!

I'm right on track!

I'm checking the time.

Get back on track!

STOP

Remember: focus on one step at a time!

COACHING TIP

LONG-TERM GOALS

For the best results with the ***Beat the Clock*** assignment, plan to keep it going for the long term. Here's how:

- Be sure to make this activity ***fun***.
- Mix it up by letting your child time you occasionally.
- Try to do it about once a day, and continue it over a long period of time.
- It may take a long time for your child to develop an accurate sense of time.
- Once you child gets used to using a timer, have your child think about when a timer might help him or her accomplish a goal.

Assignment Idea #3:
Beat the Clock!

Executive Functions
- Shifting Focus
- Emotional Control
- Internalized speech
- Inhibiting Behavior
- Initiating Behavior

RATIONALE: According to Russell Barkley, time is the "ultimate yet nearly invisible disability afflicting those with ADHD." He states that understanding time "and how one comes to organize behavior within it and toward it....is a major key to the mystery of understanding ADHD" (Barkley, 1997, pp. 337-38).

BENEFIT: This assignment is designed to help the child:
1) become more aware of the concept of the *passage of time*
2) practice estimating how much time is needed to complete a particular task or activity
3) regulate his or her actions in order to complete a set of actions within a specified period of time.

MATERIALS NEEDED:

1. Beat the Clock Score Card on **page 163.**
2. A list of possible "tasks" for the child to do.
   (Make your own list or get started with the list on page 162. Make it a mix of simple chores and "fun" things to do.)

EXPLANATION FOR CHILD:

*This assignment is called **Beat the Clock.** It will let you see how good you are at **guessing** how long it takes to do something.*

When your coach says, "It's time to beat the clock," that means it's time to play this game. You'll use this score card to keep track of how close your guesses are.

1) Your coach will choose the task and write the activity on the score card. Your coach will also tell you the maximum (the most) amount of time that can be used to finish the task.

*2) You must guess how long **you** think it will take to do the task. You can use the time the coach gives you, or–if you think it can be done faster–you can give a shorter time. Your coach will write down your **time estimate.***

3) Do the task. (You have to do it completely. If you leave a part out, your coach will ask you to continue until the task is completely done.)

*4) Your coach will then write down the **actual time** that it took you to do the task.*

5) The more you practice, the better you will get at this game.

List of activities for **Beat the Clock**

1. Set the table

2. Pick up all of the toys

3. Wash the dishes

4. Unload the groceries

5. Give the dog a bath

6. Sort cards by suit and number

7. Put together a puzzle

8. Walk around the block

9. _____

10. _____

Beat the Clock!

Task	Time Estimate	Actual Time

Task	Time Estimate	Actual Time

Beat the Clock!

Task	Time Estimate	Actual Time

Task	Time Estimate	Actual Time

Beat the Clock!

Task	Time Estimate	Actual Time

Task	Time Estimate	Actual Time

Strategies for Success: Setting Goals

The objective of the Simon Says program is to help children learn to improve their performance in everyday situations. To achieve this, the child and family make a plan to take the knowledge and skills they have learned in therapy sessions and apply them to everyday life.

Using the **Coach's Report** and the child's **Things to Do** list, goals can be put in writing. The more specific the goals, the easier it will be for the child to succeed in transferring these skills to day-to-day challenges. Examples:

General goal: *Jack will get his homework done before dinner.*

Specific goal #1: *Jack will make a game plan for the afternoon.*

Specific goal #2: *Jack will choose four Encouraging Words Cue Cards.*

Specific goal #3: *Jack will finish the game plan in one hour.*

These can be written on the Coach's Report, the child's Things to Do list, or both:

COACH'S REPORT Date_____

Child's Name _____

Coach's Name _____

If you want to SUCCEED, here are the skills that you'll NEED!

I've Got a Plan

1) Please list any significant events that have occurred since the child's last therapy session:

2) Brief description of the child's behavior, mood, etc. in the past week:

3) Do you have any specific concerns or questions today?

4) Progress toward goals
How satisfied are you with the progress you and your child are making toward therapy goals?

Goal: Jack will make a game plan for homework

Very Dissatisfied Dissatisfied Neutral - Unsure Satisfied Very Satisfied
                                                                            2

Goal: Jack will use "encouraging words" to keep himself on track.

Very Dissatisfied Dissatisfied Neutral - Unsure Satisfied Very Satisfied
-2   -1   0   1   2

Goal: Jack will use a timer to stay on track

Very Dissatisfied Dissatisfied Neutral - Unsure Satisfied Very Satisfied
-2   -1   0   1   2

Comments on goals:

Things to Do:

Name: _____

Date: _____

If you want to SUCCEED, here are the skills that you'll NEED!

I've Got a Plan

Make a game plan to help yourself get your homework done in one hour.

Write down 4 things you can say to encourage yourself to stay on track. (Or choose 4 cue cards.)

For each step on the plan, use a timer to help yourself beat the clock!

Finish your plan in one hour and have time to play!

REMEMBER:

You've got the skills that you need to succeed!

COACHING TIP

Praise and encouragement can help children work hard toward goals. **Behavior-specific praise** is more effective than **general praise**, because it reminds the child of the precise action that led to success. Even if the child has experienced only partial success, highlighting what they did correctly can help build their confidence and motivate them to continue their effort.

General praise: *Fantastic job; you got your homework done today!*

Behavior-specific praise: *Jack, this game plan you made is perfect. And you chose some good cue cards to encourage yourself. You didn't get your homework done in an hour, and you don't have time to play. I really want you to have time to play, so let's fine-tune this plan so it will work better tomorrow.*

I noticed that you didn't really pay attention to the timer until it rang. What if tomorrow, we will set the timer, and once every minute, I'll remind you how many minutes you have left. Do you think that might help? Do you want me to say the minutes out loud, or write them on a piece of paper? Are there any encouraging words you want me to say?

Strategies for Success:
Recognition and Encouragement

In this section, the child learns about *goal orientation,* learns how to make a game plan for planning and self-monitoring and practices strategies for self-motivation (encouraging words) and time management. The coach and therapist should work closely together to understand the child's needs in these areas and to plan activities that will allow the child to experience success. The coach and the therapist should work together to encourage the child's efforts in learning to use these strategies.

The *Yahoo!* materials in this section are one way to provide that recognition and encouragement as the child tries out strategies and tools to improve planning, self-monitoring and time management.

The **Yahoo!** materials include these tools:

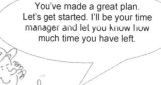

You've made a great plan. Let's get started. I'll be your time manager and let you know how much time you have left.

1. For the coach: **Encouraging Words**

This page exemplifies encouraging statements that the coach can make at the "point of performance" to acknowledge the child's progress and to direct attention, in positive ways, to areas that still need some improvement. (The therapist can also add other, more specific, statements to fit the needs of a particular child. See examples of behavior-specific praise in the Coaching Tip box on the preceding page.)

Copy the Encouraging Words page and give it to the coach as a reminder.

2. For other caretakers: **Skill Tracker**

The *Skill Tracker* form provides a way for adults other than the coach to recognize and encourage effort and progress. The form includes a copy of the *Skills Checklist* for working memory, plus a specific goal that the child is working on. For example, a grandparent, sitter or older sibling might be involved in playing "Beat the Clock." Recording the activity on the Skill Tracker reminds that child that time management is a skill that can be practiced and improved.

3. For the therapist: **Good Job! Tickets**

The therapist can provide additional incentive to complete assignments by awarding the child *Good Job!* Tickets, The tickets include the checklist of working memory skills that the child is working on, giving the therapist an opportunity to provide behavior-specific praise.

If desired, the therapist can have the child periodically "cash in" the tickets for a reward provided by the therapist. (Have a variety of rewards: inexpensive prizes and/or special activities to do at the office.)

In the *Simon Says* program, the coach:

- motivates the child by providing a vision of success.

- creates interesting (and fun!) practice sessions.

- sees that the child uses tools at the point of performance.

- **recognizes even small signs of progress and provides encouragement.**

As your child tries out strategies to help him/her **make and follow a plan**, this page gives examples of encouraging statements that you can make to point out areas of progress. You can also direct attention, in positive ways, to areas that still need some improvement.

Add other statements to fit the needs of your child, making the statements as specific as possible. In other words, don't just say *"Good job!"* Tell the child exactly what he/she did right, even if it is just a small detail. Believe that your child wants to succeed and help him/her build on each small step.

If you want to SUCCEED, here are the skills that you'll NEED!

I've Got a Plan

- ❏ Make a **PLAN** to get all of the parts done.
- ❏ Choose a way to **TRACK** your progress.
- ❏ **FOCUS** on one part at a time.
- ❏ When you finish one part, mark your progress and **SWITCH** to the next part.
- ❏ When you finish all the parts, give yourself a big *Yahoo!*

Encouraging Words

Getting started

You've come up with an excellent plan for getting the job done.

You've mapped your path to success!

Troubleshooting

I'm so glad you are eager to get started. Getting started half the battle! But, remember last time you got tired half-way through. For this job, I think if we take a few minutes to make a good plan, you will be able to pace yourself and feel really good. I'll help you.

You made a great plan. Let's get started. I'll be your time manager and let you know how much time you have left.

The plan that you made is excellent. But with such a tough job, you need a way to keep yourself motivated. Let's use the cue cards to keep you on track to success.

Recognizing effort and success

You are doing a good job of tracking your progress. With each step, you are getting closer to your goal.

You stuck with your plan and finished with time left over. That's fantastic!

Skill Tracker

Thumbs up!
for

_____
(name)

Goal: _____

Date	What happened? (Tell how the skills were used.)
_____	_____
_____	_____
_____	_____
_____	_____
_____	_____

❏ Make a **PLAN**.

❏ **TRACK** your progress.

❏ **FOCUS** on one part at a time.

❏ When you finish one part, mark your progress and **SWITCH** to the next part.

❏ Give yourself a big Yahoo!

❏ Make a **PLAN**.

❏ **TRACK** your progress.

❏ **FOCUS** on one part at a time.

❏ When you finish one part, mark your progress and **SWITCH** to the next part.

❏ Give yourself a big Yahoo!

❏ Make a **PLAN**.

❏ **TRACK** your progress.

❏ **FOCUS** on one part at a time.

❏ When you finish one part, mark your progress and **SWITCH** to the next part.

❏ Give yourself a big Yahoo!

❏ Make a **PLAN**.

❏ **TRACK** your progress.

❏ **FOCUS** on one part at a time.

❏ When you finish one part, mark your progress and **SWITCH** to the next part.

❏ Give yourself a big Yahoo!

Good Job! Tickets

Copy and cut on the dotted lines to make four tickets.

Use the tickets to reward and encourage the child's progress toward goals.

Put a checkmark by the skill (or skills) demonstrated and talk about the situation(s) in which it occurred.

This will help raise the child's awareness of the specific behaviors that are helping them to succeed!

Summary
I've Got a Plan!

Within the construct of goal orientation, the other executive functions–working memory, response inhibition and cognitive/behavioral flexibility–come together to enable the child to analyze a need, create a plan, then monitor and motivate themselves as they carry out the plan, filtering out distractions and assessing their progress. The child has also been introduced to the concept of time management, another aspect of self-monitoring that is important in achieving most goals.

Because of the complexity involved in this planning and implementing, external support is extremely important. The child has learned the strategy of using a visual aid–a game plan–to help keep in mind all of the various components. The strategy of motivating and guiding oneself with the use of internalized language has also been introduced, with external support provided by "Encouraging-Words" Cue Cards.

Some children will eventually internalize these supports. (For example they may be able to picture a game plan in their mind.) However, studies indicate that children with ADHD take longer than other children to learn, and internalize, effective self-talk. They should, therefore, be encouraged to use these (and other) external supports as long as they are needed. Many adults with ADHD report that, over the years, they learned to use regularly use a number of strategies for providing external support for their executive functions. So, the habit of planning and utilizing external support is a strategy that can serve the child well for many years.

References

Barkley, Russell A. *ADHD and the Nature of Self-Control.* The Guilford Press, 1997

Brown, Thomas. *Attention Deficit Disorder: The Unfocused Mind in Children and Adults.*
    Yale University Press, 2005.

Dutton, Judy. "How to Raise a Superstar." *ADDitude*, April, May, 2007.

Gawande, Atul. "A Lifesaving Checklist." *The New York Times,* 30 December 2007, p. 48.

Yeager, Marcie and Daniel Yeager. Executive Function & Child Development. W. W. Norton, 2013

Zelazo, Philip David. "Executive Function Part Four: Brain growth and the development of executive functio
Aboutkidshealth,
    http://www.aboutkidshealth.ca/En/News/Series/ExecutiveFunction/Pages/Executive-FunctionPart-Four-
    Brain-growth-and-the-development-of-executive-function.aspx.
    Accessed 20 November 2016.

"Activities Guide: Enhancing and Practicing Executive Function Skills with Children fFrom Infancy to
Adolescence." Center on the Developing Child: Harvard University, 2014,
    http://developingchild.harvard.edu/resources/activities-guide-enhancing-and-practicingexecutive-functio
    skills-with-children-from-infancy-toadolescence
    Accessed 20 November 2016

The **Morning DJ** technique was adapted from the *ADHD: Organizational Tips Section* of **About.com**
    http://add.about.com/cs/organizationtips
    Accessed 1 Sepember 2009

Dear Colleagues:

All of the activities in this book were developed for children and families at our clinic, *The Yeager Center for Children and Families*. We are grateful to the children and families from whom we have learned so much!

Home assignments are a critical part of the Simon Says program. Here are some suggestions for increasing compliance with therapeutic homework:

1. Put the assignment in writing. In this new edition we have provided a *Coach's Report* form and a *Things to Do* form for each section. Each form contains the skills checklist for that section, to make it easier for families to recall the goals they are working on, and tie that in with the in-session activities. Use either form or both, whichever works best for a particular family.

2. Have the child decorate a sturdy folder to transport materials for assignments.

3. **Always** check assignments as soon as the next session starts. It shows that you value the completion of assignments. Ask questions. What did the child and parent like or not like about the assignment? Do they have any suggestions to improve the assignment?

4. If the family repeatedly fails to complete assignments, schedule a time during the session to "trouble-shoot." Ask questions, find out what made it difficult to get the assignment done. Ask for suggestions to make assignments more child- and family-friendly.

5. Provide an incentive to complete assignments. Give the child a **Good Job!** *Ticket* (included in each section) for each completed assignment. The child can periodically "cash in" the tickets for a reward provided by the therapist. Have a variety of rewards: inexpensive prizes and special things to do.

We welcome your feedback as you try out these activities with your clients. We invite you to let us know what worked, what didn't work, and variations that you have used and liked.

We look forward to hearing from you!

Daniel Yeager, LCSW, RPT-S

Marcie Yeager, LCSW, RPT-S

You can reach us at: playtherapy@att.net

Daniel Yeager presents seminars based on the concepts presented in this book. For more information, contact him by phone or email.

For more therapeutic resources developed at The Yeager Center, see the next page.

Mixed Emotions: An Activity for Cognitive Behavioral

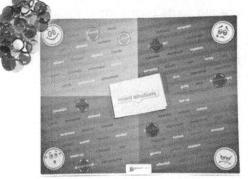

This activity includes an 11x17 folding game board, 48 color-coded chips, and 90 situation cards. The board and chips can be used for a variety of CBT activities such as a "feelings check-in" at the start of a counseling session. The cards can be added for game play. Each card presents a person confronting a situation that might evoke "mixed emotions." The persons presented include children, teens, and adults. This mixture allows players to put themselves in the place of other people, which helps players understand multiple view-points and aids in the development of empathy.

Let's THINK About Feelings: Tools for Child-Friendly CBT

Let's THINK About Feelings provides child-friendly tools for therapists who use cognitive-behavioral therapy (CBT). It is expected that therapists using this resource already have a sound theoretical understanding of CBT and a repertoire of CBT interventions that they use with clients. Let's THINK About Feelings supplements those interventions, by providing activities and visual tools that make the principles of CBT more accessible for young people.

Part 1 includes tools to help children differentiate emotions and identify stressors.

Part 2 includes tools to help children regulate emotions and behavior, focusing on response inhibition, cognitive flexibility, self-calming and self-monitoring, and problem solving. Contains dozens of reproducible tools and visually engaging worksheets

For more information about these and other resources, go to:
www.playtherapyworks.com

Made in the USA
Monee, IL
13 September 2021